Wishes

for a Mother's Heart

Wishes

for a Mother's Heart

Words of Inspiration,
Love, and Support

TRICIA LaVOICE &
BARBARA LAZAROFF

HAY HOUSE, INC.
Carlsbad, California • New York City
London • Sydney • Johannesburg
Vancouver • Hong Kong • New Delhi

Originally published by 48HrBooks: 978-0-615-34429-4

Library of Congress Control Number: 2011922464

ISBN: 978-1-4019-3534-4

14 13 12 11   4 3 2 1
1st Hay House edition, May 2011

Printed in the United States of America

FSC
Mixed Sources
Product group from well-managed
forests and other controlled sources

Cert no. SW-COC-002283
www.fsc.org
© 1996 Forest Stewardship Council

To our mothers:
Jean, Patricia, and Ellie

"Dandelion, Dandelion, with my breath
I set you free to travel the four corners
of the world where hope creates change
and change makes dreams come true."

—BARBARA

CONTENTS

John Hanwell

Tricia, Barbara, and Leeza

FOREWORD

by Leeza Gibbons

There is nothing like a mother's love. In all the world, it is unique. It endures, sustains, supports, and heals even without being asked to do so. It is the most reliable and sturdy force most of us will ever experience. Our mothers are our compasses, our sails, and anchors throughout life—guiding us, challenging us, and encouraging us as we come to the ultimate realization that we are separate from the one who gave us life. Even though we know we came through our moms to be our own people, and as mothers we let go of our children to let them find their own identities, we are connected forever in a way that feels more permanent than our time here on earth.

Maternal energy is everywhere. Being biologically bound does not make a mother . . . being heart connected does. This book is about all those who have given birth and all those who mother without ever being pregnant. It is about the strongest desires of a mother's heart and the most vulnerable corners of her soul.

This book is written *by* mothers *for* mothers. The words come in the form of *Wishes,* which are gifts we offer to ourselves and others. They are always available, they always fit, and they can be made public or kept secret. A Wish is offered with the purest intention and then released. A Wish shared between women is, in my opinion, a very sacred thing.

My good friend Tricia LaVoice began putting thoughts, feelings, and emotions in her written Wishes as a way of healing the hearts of her fellow mothers who were hurting or in pain. That's how I connected with Tricia at the play-yard where our young children went to school. She had been reaching out to her friend Barbara Lazaroff, another mom from school, through "Wishes" designed to support Barbara through a difficult time. I knew immediately that this was a special gift and should be shared. Then, my heart was broken after my marriage ended, and Tricia's soft and gentle words given to me in a Wish gave me the courage to face each new challenge.

This triangle of shared love and support was never meant to stay between us. Tricia always saw it as a circle—a sisterhood—and my part was to help open the blanket and wrap it around as many hearts as possible. I read the first Wish Tricia wrote for me, "I Wish for You, the Love of Friendship," on the air during my syndicated radio show, *Hollywood Confidential*. We have about 100 stations in the United States and Canada, and I think all three and a half million of our listeners responded to those powerful words!

"An exposed heart appreciates that which is oblivious to the secured," she wrote. She also said, "Be free to be weak." It was the beginning of my journey to recover my soul and reclaim my life.

Tricia's words elicited a huge response from my listeners, as I know they will with you. Her special and beautiful friendship with Barbara is so moving and so touching that theirs is a pairing that is stronger because of the very nature of the union.

Let Tricia's words speak to you or someone you love and then allow Barbara to help you put the Wish into action in your own life. These two friends combine their love and their talents to offer you *Wishes for a Mother's Heart*. If you keep this book for yourself, I hope you find it to be a blessing in your life, as it has been in mine. If you are giving it to someone you love, I hope the words will float like the seeds of a dandelion, landing softly where they need to be.

Love and More,

Leeza

WHAT IS A WISH?

by Barbara Lazaroff

Wishes are our heart's desires. As children we daydream, imagining what we will become, what we will look like, who we will marry, what our children will be like, and what adventures we will have. When we are quite young, we often believe we can create that perfect fantasy world by merely conjuring it up and asking for it with magical words or prayer. Sometimes we think that what we covet will find us wherever we are because we are lucky or special.

As we become more mature, most of us learn that the harder we try, the more luck we seem to have. Instead of seeking and striving with sustained hard work or education, some people feel entitled. Others become stagnant due to insecurity or failure and find it difficult to reach for their goals, afraid to stumble yet again.

Wishes are wonderful moments of fancy, and dreaming is an essential human process that has allowed for miraculous scientific discoveries, breathtaking fine art, and other masterful works of humankind. However, these realized dreams were always partnered with study or practice, knowledge and talent—all requiring enormous effort of mind, spirit, and body. To see our hopes and desires realized, we must put genuine concerted effort into taking steps to create the life we wish to live. Not unlike learning to walk or talk, raising a child, tending a garden, learning to play an instrument, or becoming a graceful dancer or a talented athlete, there is a great deal of thought, planning, practice, and failure before there is success.

One of my treasured quotes reminds us: "Courage doesn't always roar. Sometimes courage is the quiet voice at the end of the day saying, 'I will try again tomorrow.'" The Wishes in this book are meant to inspire, illuminate, touch, and motivate you to think deeply, as well as to move you viscerally. They are words that will resonate with both your mind and body. Each of you will be attracted to, and affected by, certain words, phrases, or themes; often this is very telling and highly personal.

Are you particularly moved by the Wish concerning security, comfort, loss, forgiveness, anger, or personal change? Often the Wishes will clarify and highlight for you what you are most enveloped in at that moment in your life. Always, the Wishes will reveal to you that we all share similar joys, fears, concerns, and aspirations. As you change, your attraction to certain Wishes may alter as well, but they each possess universal emotions that speak to various times in our lives that most of us can profoundly relate to, echoing our most authentic selves.

My welcome challenge is to respond emotionally to Tricia's beautiful, poetic words, and attempt to guide you in a pragmatic direction. I do so by asking you to embrace these words and insights in your heart and then transmit them to "hands" moving forward into action. I hope to provide some constructive advice on how to own a Wish with purpose and passion, and create your own personal identity and forge your own reality. Dreams are the inspiration of action, but only by taking action toward your goals can you effect real change and fulfillment in your life.

I will provide practical, creative, and dynamic solutions, opportunities, and projects to move the Wishes into the realm of substance. I want to explore some of the steps you can pursue to perhaps change your job, realize your potential, and enhance friendships and family relationships by learning to be a kinder, more compassionate and communicative individual. Be a chameleon and re-create yourself. I would like to encourage you to assemble an emotional arsenal so that you can approach every day with the attitude that "this is an exciting challenge that I will overcome with my unique skills," rather than relying on old patterns of fear of failure, believing a difficult situation is always an insurmountable obstacle.

Wishes may sound ambitious; none of us are licensed therapists, nor are our lives "perfect," whatever that would look like. Our strength and wisdom comes from our experiences and camaraderie. Thank you, Leeza, for your profoundly touching Foreword illuminating the guiding power of maternal love and your loving tribute to Jeepers, your wonderful mom. We are loving and trusting friends and mothers; we have all experienced marriage, and two have endured divorce. We have experienced losses, loves, betrayals, disappointments, triumphs, failures, and enormous change, as many women have. Tricia and I are going to share of ourselves and give the best we can to enhance, inspire, and hopefully positively influence others to expand their lives. Some of you may need to change direction; others may require techniques or inspiration to "hang in there," or move past the past—and all of us need to remember to never forget to laugh.

As resourceful, positive-thinking women, we have seen what can be accomplished with vision followed by hard work, creative solutions, redirection, personal introspection, the power of partnering, mentoring, friendship, community, love, and the will of the individual.

I will try with genuine concern to Wish and imagine along with Tricia, and to analyze and explore. I will work earnestly to engineer some of the valuable patterns and strategies one might employ to "wishimagineer" a dream come true.

> If you can dream it,
> you can do it!
> —*Barbara*

HOW THE WISHES FIRST BEGAN

by Tricia LaVoice

When I think of the Wishes and how they started, I do not know where to begin, so I will bring you back to the summer of 2005. I had just finished writing my first novel, *Pieces of My Mother* —my journey of accepting the sudden death of my mother and father twelve years earlier from an automobile accident. After the death of my parents, two very special women came into my life, offering me the unconditional love and support I needed to restore my faith and trust in life, allowing me to be the mother and wife I wished to be for my family. I questioned if my mother had sent them to me. Barbara Lazaroff was one of those women who became family to me.

As all of us do, Barbara had her share of hardships. September of 2005 brought with it some new challenges, and Barbara was not anticipating that the month would be a good one. She had been such a loving and supportive friend as I wrote my manuscript, on top of making my four children feel special. It was my turn to give back to her. As we sat on her back patio that late August afternoon, I pledged to be a noncomplaining friend devoid of all issues and problems the whole month of September. "In fact," I suggested, "I will not only be the best listener in the world, I will 'wish' you something every night."

So that is how it started—good listening skills followed by a simple e-mail saying, "Good morning" or "Good night," depending on how promptly I could get to my computer, with a simple

Wish: "Today, September 1, 2005, I wish for you Trust or Compassion, and so on. However, shortly into the month, life reminded us how fragile and unforeseen it can be. On September 6, Hurricane Katrina hit the American coast, causing unfathomable damage. On September 8, my husband informed me that we would need to relocate to the Hartford area of Connecticut. And, in the early morning of September 11, I was woken up by the phone. My sister's voice was telling me to come home. Her son—my nephew, Aaron—had tragically died at the age of nineteen. Again, Barbara became support for me and my family. I continued writing Wishes as an outlet during the week I spent with my sister and her family. Upon returning to Los Angeles, September continued on its path of uncertainty. Barbara experienced some unexpected medical troubles along with personal issues to accompany the problems she faced. Over the month, the Wishes became personal and profound, documenting the events that unfolded.

At the time, Leeza's children attended the same school as Barbara's and mine. I spoke with her only occasionally, but I was always comforted by her kindness and sincerity. How it came about that I spoke to her on the play-yard and frantically divulged the month's heartbreaks, I do not know. In my frenzy, I also told her about writing Wishes for Barbara, and how I was documenting the month in a way I could never have imagined in August. That night, Leeza sent me an e-mail, a Wish for peace in my life. This was the start of our friendship. Over the next months, I found a treasured trust and loyalty in Leeza—a sisterhood—as if we had been friends all our lives.

I stayed in Los Angeles and finished out the school year with the children, as my husband dutifully commuted back and forth from the East Coast. Leaving California and the comfort of all my friends was, to say the least, very difficult for me. My nephew's death and the painful memories it dug up made me that much more dependent on my friends Barbara and Leeza for support. I left Los Angeles that summer brokenhearted. In September 2006, I wrote Wishes once more, but they lacked luster as I struggled to adjust and acclimate four children into a new lifestyle.

During my first year in Connecticut, I faced one of the toughest times of my life. Simply put, I was miserable. My husband was working hard at a new position and away from home a lot. The children were off at school trying to make new friends. I spent much of my time alone, something I had never done before in my life. Although I still spoke to Barbara and Leeza and other friends, it was hard to maintain the same level of friendship without the day-to-day involvement. My life experiences had left me with the fear of loss, and I struggled to hold on to my friendships—people I considered family—but that is hard to do with 3,000 miles between you. I cannot tell you if, had I not lost so many family members unexpectedly, my friends would have mattered so much to me. Life certainly challenges all of us in one way or another, and most people need friends to help them. I certainly did.

It was the first time since my parents' death, and Aaron's death, that I was alone with my thoughts. I had no choice but to confront the pain in front of me and walk right through it. I had never felt so alone, but I am a survivor and yearned for peace and happiness. I began taking long walks and sorting through all my thoughts. As the summer reached an end, I was unsure if I would write Wishes, but come September 1, I sent one off to Barbara. By September 6, she had recognized that my time alone had offered me insight and suggested I share the Wishes with others. Later in the month, I met Leeza in Manhattan while she was there working on a Sheer Coverage photo shoot. I mentioned to her that I was writing Wishes again. Leeza loved the concept and encouraged me to write beyond September. As time went on, I began writing Wishes for all the people in my life. Then, in late October, while searching through a box that had gotten misplaced in the shuffle, I found a light blue leather pouch that Leeza had given me two years earlier, containing a pretty pair of earrings. Embroidered across the pouch read the word *wish*. It was then that we knew it was time to print these Wishes.

These Wishes are my thoughts stemming from all the love in my life from my husband, children, sisters, friends, and from all the love my parents gave me while they were with me. These Wishes also stem from all the pain I have endured in my life, which has opened my heart to greater depths, allowing me to appreciate that love. They belong to all and confirm that the greatest gift—the most powerful force the universe has to offer us—is that of human kindness.

Love,

Wishes

for the Heart

We gave careful consideration to dividing this chapter into two sections: Wishes for the Mother's Heart and Wishes for the Child's Heart; however, we elected to leave it as one. In every mother's heart lies a child in need of love and support. Every mother is someone's daughter, and she is deserving of maternal love all of her life.

For You, I Wish

The Beauty of a Dandelion

"Let her be," I heard the older child whisper to the younger.
"Please!"
"No, she's resting."
I lie half-awake, nursing a headache as my children congregate outside my door. Time passes and again I hear their voices.
"Now?"
"No."
Curiosity over my child's impatience and excitement prevail, so I call out for him to come. He runs to my bedside yelling, "Mommy, Mommy, look! I picked you a beautiful flower." The proud twinkle in his eyes accompanies his smile, which starts in his heart and travels through his tender seven-year-old body before exploding onto his face. He opens up his tightly gripped fingers and lays a freshly picked dandelion beside me.

The dandelion, labeled a weed in science books, is discarded from our gardens and rarely set on our tables. I pick up the white fluffy gift and search for a scent I know is not there. I think of you, knowing that you are feeling discarded and unappreciated at this juncture of your life. My vision holds a different view, though. I remember your laughter like a field of daisies and see your smile in a bundle of sunflowers. I look to you and see the grace of a lily, the complexity of an orchid, the sweetness of a lilac. But my image of you holds little importance without your acknowledgment.

Like you, the beauty of the dandelion lies deeper than the eye can see. It allows itself to need the grace of others for survival, calling on the soil for nourishment, the rain to quench its thirst, and the sun to warm its petals.

So let the words of those you love be your soil and nourish your soul. Let the compassion of others be your rain and quench your thirst for love. Let their laughter be your sun and warm your heart. Allow yourself to need and be needed.

"My vision holds a different view."

—Tricia LaVoice

❋ Reflection ❋

There are many windows in our home, and there's a different view of our yard depending on which window one is looking out of. My bedroom window overlooks a big tree that is bare all winter long, blossoms in spring, and then remains beautifully green the rest of the year. My youngest son requested to leave the spray-painted snow from the holidays on his windows all year long, and then the windows in the family room are always a bit dusty, either from my poor housekeeping skills or a wind that must continually blow dust on that side of the house. Each window in our home frames a distinct view, but the yard itself remain constant. Life is a bit like this, too. Our perception of our world, regardless of what is reality, is what influences our thoughts the most. Of course, circumstance comes into play and it is much easier to have positive thoughts when life is being kinder to you.

My one dear friend Sheila and I talk every Monday morning to catch up after the weekend. She lives by the beach in Los Angeles and I live in the woods in Connecticut. During the winter months, many Mondays are freezing and gray in Connecticut and I will be feeling disheartened, while Sheila will sound chipper as she walks her dog along the pier in 70-degree weather. Sometimes she has to remind me that once the sun shines and the flowers blossom, things will look different.

It is important to recognize the outside forces that are affecting your thoughts, and separate them from how you are truly feeling. Perception, just like the weather, can change; but unlike the weather, our perception is in our control. Change your thoughts and the whole world changes. It is much easier to change our thoughts than we may think. Like any bad habit, negative thinking can be corrected when exercised.

Leeza is so very generous with her compliments to me, and periodically she will mail me words of encouragement, telling me what a wonderful person she thinks I am. I pin them up on my vision board and know my family will read them, thinking Leeza has no idea that I am not nearly as sweet as she believes. My behavior may come off as sweet, but my thoughts can be negative before I massage them to be kinder. It is important for me to see my world lovingly and peacefully. When I catch myself thinking negatively about something, I try to pull my thoughts over to the positive. The more I practice positive thinking, the easier it is to envision my world as a kinder and gentler place and, as a result, the kinder and gentler my world becomes.

Having a positive perception is never more vital than when perceiving yourself. But who are you? Are you who YOU think you are or are you how other people perceive you to be? Everyone in the world can think we are wonderful, but if we do not believe that, none of it matters; it is our perception of ourselves that matters.

As mothers, having a healthy perception of ourselves is imperative since our children are sensitive to our sense of self-worth. Children will gain their own self-worth and strength from a mother who likes herself and, most important, respects herself. But it is easy to think negatively of oneself and, for that reason, it takes less effort. On the other hand, it takes courage, confidence, and action to think positively, and we must always remember that our children are watching how we act and will emulate what they observe.

Writing this book makes my heart grow, but having the courage to get it to you is a challenge for me. I have a message from Barbara, whose note sits next to Leeza's note on my vision board, that reads: "I Wish you the realization that perseverance does spawn victory and success. I Wish you the realization that you are your own mirror, that what you project, you must first believe for others to believe it as well." I read those words when I need a little encouragement, but I gain most of my courage to believe in myself when one of my children says something encouraging about my writing. When I see them believing in me, I know I cannot let them down. I believe so they can believe.

"We are not born equal, we are born unique. We must learn to celebrate our matchless qualities; share our distinctive inner radiance, warming all we touch with our time on this earth."

—Barbara Lazaroff

Words and Actions from Barbara

The dandelion is actually many delicate, tiny flowers gathered together. Each of these tiny flowers produces a seed attached to a stem with white fluffy threads; one portion is curiously called a "wishie"! As a child they delighted me; with my breath I had the power within me to send these fluffy messengers of my fanciful notions off to places unknown. As I watched them gracefully fluttering away, I was joyful and anticipatory. I suggested the dandelion as our Wishes' visual and spiritual talisman and was certain that once the dandelion was fittingly remembered with beloved childhood feelings (rather than as the adult gardener's commonplace lawn nuisance), it could resume its rightful honor as a magical wand of childlike empowerment! As with so many things in life, the dandelion's image and worth was all a matter of perspective.

- *Start by deciding you are uniquely able, and affirm that you are a valuable person. (List your assets, skills, talents, and what you appreciate about yourself; ask others what they find distinctive about you.)*

- *You need to confirm that you are who you know ourselves to be, not how others alone see you. (Your self-worth should be determined by character and spirit, not by what car you drive or what purse you carry. People sometimes make poor character and worth assessments about others in this celebrity-driven, monetary society; your value should not be determined by how others with shallow ideals treat you. If you are kind, respectful, honest, hard-working, a good citizen, and a concerned family member, you are indeed a person of enormous substance!)*

- *If you want the world to truly see you, you must open that window to yourself, allowing others to view the beauty and wisdom you hold within.*

- *You do not need a complete makeover to feel renewed. Start with the simplest yet most important of elements: smile. People will smile back.*

- *Say "hello"; people will respond, and you will feel immediately more connected to the world around you.*

- *Practice self-reflection. What do you like about yourself? Learn to meditate, think deeply, and find a place where you can be silent. (These are examples of an internal process.) What would you like to change or improve? Perhaps keep a journal of your likes and dislikes, and a plan for self-improvement: additional schooling or professional training, exercise, and mindful eating, such as healthier cuisine and portion control. (This is an action project, both short- and long-term.)*

- *Create a personal self-affirming mantra (something as simple as: "I am wonderful and valuable," or "I can do it," or "Today I will . . ." and decide what you will work toward for this day.)*

- *You must be ready for the change or it will not be effective. You must decide you want to change and are ready to meet the consequences of your transformation. It will be hard work. You will discover that the greater the change, the more time and effort you must exert. Perhaps it will take years of study, vigorous exercise, or an unpaid internship, but you need to commit to persevering.*

The following lines are extracted from Nelson Mandela's 1994 inaugural speech, but they were actually written by author Marianne Williamson in her book *A Return to Love*. This is one of my favorite mantras. I recommend looking it up and reading it in its full glory:

"Our deepest fear is not that we are inadequate. Our deepest fear is that we are powerful beyond measure. It is our light, not our darkness that frightens us . . . It's not just in some of us; it is in every one. And as we light our own, we unconsciously give other people permission to do the same."

Beauty in Your Distinctive Way

Enchantment, the exuberant diversity in a field of wildflowers;
    Aromatic harmony, staccato essences.
    Silken, velvet, prickly, translucent tissue fine; youthful, moist
    sensual pizzicato textures trill as they are plucked and pulled.
The poised chorus line, not in line, but dotted across the verdant stage,
    Captured in place, at repose, beautiful but not free
    Liberated by hand to a jar to linger,
    Admired, adored, but gone too soon, too fragile to remain.
    Stronger in the earth.
The quiet dandelion whispers, "Come to me, come closer,
    With your life-breath scatter me to the wind so that I might travel
    See the world; share my magic with all the flowers of the field."
    Modest dandelions; graceful dancers, arabesque, plié, relevé,
    as they float away.
Skybound they glance below, the wildflowers lean and sway,
    some standing tall, others bending to the winds, some begin to bow.
Dandelion, you have found beauty in your distinctive way.

— BARBARA LAZAROFF

For You, I Wish

Trust

I love you, yes, you know this. However, I search my heart to like you in this moment. I call on myself for compassion and patience to understand you, yet I am challenged by my wounded heart. In your time of turmoil you shut your doors, build windowless walls, and retreat to your cave. I must respect your choice, but you have stayed away too long, and loved ones hurt in your departure from them.

Adversity spares no one, and we are all deserving of our healings and dealings. However, we are social creatures, webs of emotion touching one another with our joys and sorrows, and must remain accountable to one another. The line between self-evolvement and responsibility is fine. We search books and worship, turn to dependencies for relief, neglecting to look for clarity in the one place it may rest most.

To emerge from your place of pain, to find answers to your questions, you must start from within. You do not dare do so, for you fear what you will see; I understand, it is scary. Our hardships are our greatest teachers, but our vision is blurred if we do not look to understand the pupil.

I remain loyal to you, holding up the bridge that connects you to me, but I fear my arms are weakening. I will not abandon you, for unconditional love will not allow it.

Put down your walls, emerge from your cave, and trust that human kindness is waiting for you. For you, I wish trust.

"I will not abandon you,
for unconditional love
will not allow it."

—Tricia LaVoice

❋ Reflection ❋

This Wish was actually written for a very good friend of mine who was going through a difficult time in her life. We chose to include it in the mother's collection due to the response we received from Leeza's listeners. Mothers of both male and female teenagers wrote that they gave the Wish to their teenagers in the hopes of opening some form of communication with their children.

Every time my heart starts to pound and my stomach flip-flops with worry that there is something wrong with my teenagers, I ask myself: Why do they get so emotional? Why do I have to ask them a hundred times to do something? How can they talk to me that way? Will they ever be able to handle a job or any responsibility? After I ask myself all those questions, and more, I remind myself that bookstores are crawling with books on raising teenagers, so I must not be the only one worrying.

There is a great need to protect our teenagers from the world around them as well as from themselves. It baffles me that teenagers do not have better control of their impulses, as if survival of the fittest would have corrected that human flaw by now. But until they are young adults, their brains are still developing and they will make decisions that could be harmful to them. They become more independent as they grow, fighting for their freedom, yet they need us now to guide and protect them as much as ever before. The difficulty is that our children do not think they need us and they shut us out.

Breaking through the silence is difficult because many teenagers can be stubborn and do not think we know what we are talking about. They are not always wrong. Many times, we may hear our children, but we are not listening to them. We think we know what it is like being a teenager since we have all been one. However, as my wonderful friend Sheila enlightens me, "We may have been teenagers, but we have no idea what it is like to be a teenager in today's world."

At first, I thought this applied only to boys who go into their caves and don't share any of their problems with us. My daughter, Olivia, shares so much with me I sometimes wish she had a cave, and my teenage son gives me the same answer to every question: "Fine." When talking to other parents, it seems to be an issue with both sexes during the teenage years. In anticipation that one day my teenagers would shut me out, I did my best to begin dialoguing with them early and consistently. Every night I tried to lie down with each child and talk to them in the privacy of their rooms. I thought this gave them a safe place to open up to me and was hopeful this would continue into their teenage years. Nevertheless, what I have found is that they stay up later than I stay up and they would rather be on Facebook or on the phone with a friend than lie down with me.

Getting teenagers to open up is not easy, and getting them to self-reflect and take responsibility can be almost impossible. But, to ensure healthy relationships throughout their lives, communication skills must be taught just like teaching the ABCs. Unfortunately, schools do not have the budget to teach Feeling and Expressing Your Emotions 101, so the job falls solely on us.

Ah, the charm of raising teenagers—the moments you are not plagued with frustration are actually fun and exciting.

❋ ❋ ❋

Words and Actions from Barbara

When recently reading this headline on the cover of a magazine: "Friends Don't Let Friends Stay Depressed," I thought about the challenge of respecting someone's wishes for privacy, and knowing when to step in; that point of equilibrium can be delicate. A few years ago a very dear friend was going through a divorce and "locked" herself away in her bedroom for over a year. I would call and call, but she would not answer. A group of us took turns going to her home, sitting with her and bringing her food. One of our friends would simply leave a meal on her doorstep and call her to let her know it was there. I was very close to her, and being terribly concerned, I finally got a little more assertive with her. At first I would bring her into the bathroom and have her brush her hair, then ask her to put on a little makeup before taking her for a ride; and eventually insisted we go out to lunch, a movie, or window shop. A friend can be trusted to intervene, to support, to listen.

- *Stay consistent with your calls. Being dependable creates an atmosphere of trust.*

- *Send a "Good Morning!" text every day. Try not to miss a day; do the best you can.*

- *You could use your cell phone to take pictures of the beautiful outdoors and send them off to brighten your friend's day, especially if she is confined to the indoors.*

- *Sit quietly with your friend (or call), and genuinely listen. Try not to interrupt. Take a cue if she wants advice or conversation. When people tell you about a problem or concern, they are not necessarily asking, nor ready, to hear your advice or "solution."*

- *Suggest going for a walk. If possible, set up a regular time. If your friends ask how you are doing, share your news, but do not burden them with your hardships unless you have shared the type of relationship that is deeply honest and you feel they want to hear the details and can cope with them. Occasionally it helps to empower friends who are not feeling in control of their own situations if you share a problem they can help you with.*

- *A troubled or ill friend may care about you but may be too vulnerable to absorb any more difficulty; use your insight and best judgment.*

- *Make sure your friends are getting proper nutrition. People who are in crisis mode, such as depression, or who are physically ill, need to adhere to certain practices such as mindful eating and refraining from a high intake of sugar, alcohol, and refined carbohydrates. A supportive program such as taking omega 3 supplements, vitamin D, Bs, chromium, calcium, magnesium; and other minerals, vitamins, and nutrients are essential to sustaining a healthy system, and even more essential for one that is stressed and depleted. These elements can be found in fresh whole-food products (many packaged foods often have high levels of sodium, preservatives, dyes, and corn syrup, and should be avoided). Fresh fruits, vegetables, fish, lean meats (in moderation if you consume meat) will greatly support the distressed mind and body.*

- *Make sure your friend is getting at least eight hours of sleep plus daily sunlight and exercise. Try suggesting that she practice relaxation techniques. You might even practice together. As a temporary or long-term caretaker you likely need rejuvenation as well. Try biofeedback or yoga.*

- *Spending time in nature, and playing with a pet, can help lower blood pressure, and raise levels of endorphins (the "feel good" hormones). All this and sharing time with positive, comforting people increases a person's general feeling of well-being. Ask other friends if they can rotate days with you to share the love, concern, and responsibility.*

- *Noting your thoughts, activities, and aspirations in a journal helps to provide a sense of a measurable accomplishment. Bring your friend an attractive journal, and ask her to share her thoughts. She may want to keep them private, so respect that decision.*

- *Suggest she do something spontaneous, or novel—either alone, or better yet, with a friend or a group of friends at first. Sharing time with positive, comforting people increases a person's general feeling of well-being. Remember, if you are not a trained psychologist, and if you feel that someone's depression or illness is severe and not improving, help your friend seek professional care.*

"It has been said that to be trusted is a greater compliment than to be loved. I can understand this.

With trust there is respect; without respect and trust there cannot be a genuine and abiding love."

—BARBARA LAZAROFF

For You, I Wish

My Love and Gratitude

Life holds precious gifts for us, unfolding as we call upon them. All are treasures, yet there is one that has immeasurable value. This gift is living within the essence of all women, regardless of age, or whether they have given birth or not—it is the gift to nurture, to value, to bestow maternal love. I ask, but what is a mother? She is the one who lifts you when your heart is aching, the one who finds you when you have lost "you," the one who stands silent so you can sing. She cares for you in illness, celebrates you in triumph, and encourages you in hardship.

You are my friend; when I am down, you lift me up, when I am lost, you find me, and when I achieve, you celebrate me. I wish for you my love and gratitude.

"Whether our mothers are living down the street or are no longer with us, at all ages, our girlfriends offer us support and love. I am surrounded by loving women who offer me the ability to be more loving, and for that I am incredibly thankful."

—TRICIA LaVOICE

❊ Reflection ❊

It was early April last year when I was walking through the card section at Costco and the prettiest floral card caught my eye. I picked it up and began to read the beautiful devotion on the cover when I suddenly realized that it was a Mother's Day card. Quickly, I returned it to the shelf, trying to block out the sad feelings that overcome me when I accept that I am no longer able to mail my mother such cards. But as I continued shopping, I could not stop thinking about the card. It was that pretty, and I thought about what it really means to send a Mother's Day card. That is when I decided to send a card to all the women in my life who had loved me, celebrated me, and stood still for me when I needed their support.

At all ages, our women friends offer us special support and love, whether our mothers are living down the street or are no longer with us, I am surrounded by loving women. I like to think about how women lived together in biblical times, and even now all over the world, in tribes. Together, they run villages, feed and nurture the children and men, attend to the sick and more, but they do it together, offering one another emotional support that replenishes them and provides the strength to continue giving to all who depend on them.

In modern society, we are spread out, living separately in our own homes, raising our own families, but that does not mean that the bond between women is any less important. I used to worry that I gave too much time to my friends when we lived in Los Angeles. Although I was with my children the majority of the time, I would be talking with my friends, engaged in conversation while the children played. At school events, I worried that I socialized more than I paid attention to the events at hand. So when we moved to the quiet suburbs of Connecticut, I thought the isolation with my children would be good for my family. It was not. As I took care of their needs, I came to find that without the girlfriend lunches, the girlfriend walks on the beach, and the shared cups of tea, I was tired and cranky.

Once, when I was complaining to a friend that I was lonely living in Connecticut, she asked, "How could you be lonely? You are surrounded by kids and a loving husband." I did not bother to defend myself, for I knew she had never had the experience of moving to a town devoid of close girlfriends and, therefore, could not appreciate what I was feeling. I did adjust to being in Connecticut without my friends, but I think my whole family will agree that it was not until I opened myself up to meeting new people to walk and talk and drink tea with that I returned to my whole, happy self.

Last year I sent a Mother's Day card to a couple of special women who have always been maternal in their love to me, always making sure I am taking care of myself. I sent a card to my mother-friends of all ages to give them support and to thank them for _their_ support. I sent one to each of my sisters, one to my mentor, and I sent one to my girlfriends who never gave birth but who were just as loving in their friendship. Although I am not able to send my mother a card on Mother's Day, I recognize that I am surrounded by loving women who offer me the ability to be more loving, and for that I am incredibly thankful.

Words and Actions from Barbara

Try demonstrating gestures of love more often; people need to connect on a more human level, particularly in this era of ever-increasing technology. I often gift my friends with distinctly personal expressions of my love: words of support by calling often, writing to them on carefully selected or handmade cards, remembering their favorite scents or flowers, making ceramic objects for them, writing them loving or amusing poems, finding small objects they collect, or taking them to events I know they will enjoy. Some of my friends have lost their mothers years ago; others are struggling with their mom's illness, as I am now; and some girlfriends have never experienced a close enough maternal connection.

I learned to demonstrate my care in this manner by seeing my own mother's joyful response to my naïve and simple offerings of love and gratitude when I was young. My mother's fondest gifts from me as a child were not purchased, but rather created with my heart, mind, and hands: an anniversary poem I composed and painted on a rock, Mother's Day prose: "Beauty, My Mother's Glowing Face," which hangs on the kitchen wall (no matter how many times we have moved); and the albums of my sons' births, their beloved grandsons! My parents adored the videos, and the endless weekly photos I sent them of their grandsons as they grew, allowing them to "see" the boys mature from across the country.

Some of my most valued possessions include cards my boys wrote and illustrated, and their drawings and clay work from school, all of which I recognize as masterpieces! Most precious are my tender memories of their hugs, kisses, and deliciously unabashed words of affection and abiding love. Some of the most significant moments are how we always said "I love you" when my sons and I would speak to my mom and dad on the phone. Since they have moved nearby, there is never a "Good-bye" without an "I love you." My beau never ends a call without expressing love, and when we are apart, he calls me often for no other reason than to say the words.

We can support other women who do not have their own mothers present by mothering them with all the love that is around to share; we all have enough within us to go around to create a circle of friendship wherein our sisters feel cherished. As we give of ourselves, we receive and are replenished with love and gratitude.

- *The spoken word is the greatest gift. Just say how you feel. Think about the joy and comfort your friends and family receive from your warm words. If you are not naturally an expressive person, try practicing words of love and support. You may feel awkward at first; however, the positive rewards of closer relationships will ease that initial self-consciousness.*

- *Handwrite a letter of appreciation. Try to include details about your friend's loving nature and her gift of friendship.*

- *Take pictures of her garden or yours, a family pet, her children, a car she is proud of, a funny or memorable moment from your friendship. Frame them, or make greeting cards with the images. Although I never go anywhere without my camera, these photo-cards are Tricia's specialty! She has photographed every variety of rose bush in my garden and sends me notes on the cards she makes. She feels I don't take enough time to enjoy my roses.*

- *Bring over flowers for no other reason than to brighten her day.*

- *Simply make your friend a cup of tea or a sandwich and spend a little time sharing; these little acts of kindness nourish the soul, both for you and your friend.*

- *If you are seeking a grander gesture than flowers, arrive with a small tree and plant it together. You can do research on the internet or at the library on the symbolism behind a specific tree to help you make a meaningful selection. For example, Tricia sent me a Western Redbud tree that blossoms in springtime with purple flowers, my favorite color. This tree has unique heart-shaped leaves that she felt represented our devoted friendship. She included lovely words that were soothing and uplifting. Her creative gift is timeless, and I was extremely touched.*

"The loneliest woman in the world is a woman without a close woman friend."

—GEORGE SANTAYANA,
A MAN OF LETTERS
(TRUE, AND WRITTEN BY A MAN NO LESS!)

When I was nine years old I composed this poem
for my mom as a Mother's Day gift.

Beauty, My Mother's Glowing Face

Beauty is a flower with dew on every petal,
Where bees who gather honey may pick this place to settle.

Beauty is a meadow, a flawless paradise,
One place God meant for everyone;
For beauty has no price.

Beauty is someone to love, someone to stand beside;
Who with you, would walk the earth,
Or cross the ocean wide.

Beauty is innocence,
Intelligence,
And grace;
But most of all, beauty is,
My mother's glowing face.

Love, Barbara

For You, I Wish

The Village Well

There is a well where the children go to quench their infinite thirst; their thirst for love and safety, patience and acceptance; their endless needs for confidence, reassurance, direction, trust, and respect. This well I speak of I call "You." A hole below the surface of the earth or a spring bursting with purity—no matter what you call it, you are responsible for gathering the strength to quench the boundless thirst of your young. Some days your water overflows with abundance, yet on other days your well runs dry. Like the water that sustains your children's young bodies, the water from your well is essential to their being. There are no days off and the children, young and old, are not yet required to replenish what they take. So where do you go, what do you do, when the depth and quality of your well water runs short? Thankfully, wells are meant to be shared by all in the village.

When you tire, let your children come to my well. When I tire, welcome my children to yours. Together, we can serve all those in need. For you, I wish the village well.

"I can think of no more beautiful
gift a friend can give to another friend
than to love her children and help make
a positive difference in their lives."

—Tricia LaVoice

❋ Reflection ❋

Extended family is a wonderful source of love and support to help promote a child's self-esteem, build character, and instill values. But in today's world, many of us do not live close to our extended families. My family and Rich's family are very supportive of our kids; however, throughout most of our married lives, we have not lived near either of our families. We have therefore found ourselves relying on friends for added support.

Like the wish says, "There are no days off." The day I found out I was pregnant with Olivia, our first child. I became a mother. I felt vulnerable and responsible. From that moment on, in everything I did, I thought of her first. I remember that day and think about how many days I have had off from that responsibility since the day she was born, and I keep coming up empty-handed. Sure, we can go away on vacation or just out for the night, but no matter whom we leave in charge—our parents, our best friends, or even the Super Nanny—we never stop being the mommy—the one they will call if there is a problem, the one they want if they are scared or need loving. We never stop loving and worrying about them. We may get a break from dinner and bedtimes every now and then, but emotionally there are no breaks.

I love nothing more than being the mother, the mommy, but there are days that I just do not have the emotional energy to be parenting the way I want to. There are some days I just want to yell, "Because I said so!" and I do. The boys will respond to my unwarranted yelling, but it seems to backfire on me with Olivia. I can yell at her five days in a row to clean her room, to no avail, but if I speak softly while acknowledging that I understand it is not fun, yet would she please pick up her room, she will get to it much sooner and without the drama. On the days that I am tired and become reactive in my parenting instead of proactive, I greatly appreciate help from my closest friends. Helping one another out with car-pooling, sleepovers, or dinner is an essential part of tag-team mothering. However, going that extra step, being actively involved with one another's children, can make all the difference.

Barbara knows how irritable I can become when helping my children with their math homework. Many times, on the days Barbara picked my kids up from school, I would find her sitting with one of them, helping them with their math. And then there are the talks that kids seem to pay more attention to when they come from an adult other than their own parent. My heart melts when I hear one of my friends asking my children about their hobbies or school. The children seem to bask in the interest of another adult and eagerly share their thoughts and stories. Recently, Leeza sat with Olivia to talk about a future in journalism. I watched as Olivia took in every word, and I found myself reveling in and appreciating the way Leeza's love and friendship was making a difference in my daughter's life.

Mothering is the most rewarding job a woman can have, yet it is not always easy. I can't think of a more beautiful gift a friend can give to another friend than to love her children and help make a positive difference in their lives.

Words and Actions from Barbara

The next time you find yourself about to say, "Let me know if I can be of help," stop, reflect, and truly extend yourself by spontaneously doing just that: act! Remember that "the smallest act of kindness is worth more than the grandest intention." Mothers must support one another; we can help in so many vital ways because we understand other mothers' issues in such intimate ways.

The African proverb "It takes a whole village to raise a child" is profound. It certainly requires a community of women to support each other so we can uphold our never-ending commitments to those we love and our sometimes overwhelming obligations to family, friends, work, and community. Perhaps we can ease that sense of fragmentation women often feel: that we can never do enough, or fulfill everyone's expectations of us. If we try to band together and collaborate on some daily tasks and/or long-range projects, though, we can accomplish much.

- *If you are going somewhere, even just to the grocery store, offer to take a tired mom's child along with you.*

- *Help your friend's children with their homework, read to them, or ask them to read to you. I have done this often with friends, and it is always deeply appreciated. (This is where I have stepped in for Tricia numerous times.) I have actually learned and relearned a great deal myself (patience, as well as history, math, an interpretative review of Shakespeare, and a realization that I have forgotten a great deal of my years of university-level chemistry and biology, and I'm embarrassed to admit some of my elementary grammar as well!).*

- *Offer to host a friend's child's birthday party. One of my fondest memories was creating an English garden tea party for Tricia's daughter Olivia's thirteenth birthday. My garden is a gorgeous faux English mélange of aromatic flowers and trees. The young ladies dined on scones and clotted cream, little finger sandwiches, and decadent desserts. The beautiful table décor was composed of roses I cut and arranged from my garden, and all the girls wore hats! You can simplify this and the girls will still have a grand time! Be imaginative; have the ladies create hats from cardboard boxes, wrapping paper and ribbons; and award a few prizes for the silliest, strangest, loveliest, and most dramatic creations. An indoor tea party with petite individual flowers, perhaps tiny tea roses that the girls can each take home, would thrill them.*

- *When calling a friend's house, talk to her children about school and sports. Express genuine interest. When you discover their passions, suggest an outing; perhaps you know an expert in that area—a scientist, actor, professor, doctor, attorney, talent agent, film maker, chef, businesswoman, or an athlete with whom they could meet or exchange a letter or e-mail with for inspiration.*

- *Consider taking a friend's child on your family vacation or over-night to give her a respite. Last year my girlfriend was undergoing chemotherapy and wanted her son to enjoy his spring break; although we would miss sharing the annual trip with her, it was my profound joy to take her son (who is good friends with my younger son), along for the vacation. This gesture eased her greatly, and she could concentrate on her health.*

- *If permitted, attend a school conference or doctor's appointment for your friend's child when she truly cannot make these important appointments and needs the extra support.*

- *Attend a school function, like Grandparent's Day, for a friend's children if they do not have grandparents living in the area, or they have passed away. This is something I would do almost every year for Tricia's children since her parents are both deceased. When my parents were in town, they would attend and be the "elder friends."*

- *Help your friend's children make a special birthday surprise or Mother's Day gift for their mother. Thank you, Tricia, for all the terrifically clever surprises you created with my sons to delight me, make me laugh, and help them feel great about their demonstrations of love.*

"Many people will walk in and
out of your life, but only true friends
will leave footprints on your heart."

—ELEANOR ROOSEVELT, FORMER FIRST LADY

"Don't ask, what can I do?
Do something, do it with
heart, and do it now."

—BARBARA LAZAROFF

For You, I Wish

My Care

I walked in the weather today feeling the soft droplets of rainfall on my grateful face. Rain, a weeping of the sky releasing months of matter held high in the clouds until she can hold back no longer. I welcomed her downpour, for Mother Nature has worked diligently, turning the hardships of winter into a rainbow of color for those she loves.

I thought of you as I walked. I heard your concerned voice ask me, "Who takes care of you, my friend?" You place kudos on my doorstep and show appreciation for my words. Then you move to the next in need and place your arms there. Before retiring, you reach for one more weary soul, finally retreating to your own dwelling, where children await their share of your love and affection. The role of the caretaker, the concierge to their world, squeezed between the young and the old, responsible for generations past and present filled with rewards, yet not getting easier with age.

Now I ask you, my friend, who takes care of you? Are the clouds behind your eyes filled to capacity, wanting their own downpour? Do you fear letting go and flooding those you love? I watch you turn the hardships of your world into rainbows of color. I watch you nurture those young and old, care for the generations past and present. I wake to my world some days with the arms of an octopus, other days with clouds behind my eyes ready to burst, but if you can take my love, my friendship, my loyalty, rain or shine, I reach my hand to you in care. For you, I wish my care.

"Who takes care of you, my friend?"

—Tricia LaVoice

"Sometimes all we need is a
good cry and just a little love."

—Tricia LaVoice

❋ Reflection ❋

Who takes care of you?

I asked five of my closest friends this question and got a variety of answers. Sadly, one of them whom I have known forever and talk to every day, replied, "@#%* NOBODY." I think that was a message that I needed to pick her up some groceries and take her kids for the weekend. I loved Barbara's answer because I watch her try to save the world, so when she replied with multiple names, I was pleased. She also has the most devoted "manfriend" (she hates the term "boyfriend") a woman could ask for; and wonderful, loving parents.

However, my exhausted friend above, as with many of my friends, has teenagers she is raising and now aging parents who need her support, and is going through a divorce. My parents were both in their mid-fifties and healthy when they died—they were still in the giving seat. I have not experienced the sandwich stage, but I watch my friends as they juggle the roles of mothering children and being a caretaker for aging parents. It is a stage that most mothers experience, and if we think back to when we were young, we can remember our mothers caring for our grandmothers. Unfortunately, women no longer gather around the fire and share responsibilities, supporting one another while the men hunt. Most of us, regardless of whether we're taking care of parents or family or work or friends, understand how overextending ourselves can build up and make us feel like the tree in the children's book <u>The Giving Tree,</u> just like an old stump with nothing more to offer than for someone to sit on us.

I wrote this Wish for Leeza two years ago when she was going through a divorce and her mother was still alive with Alzheimer's. She is always so kind to me and is always asking me who takes care of me. Yet, I watch her give and give and give, desperately trying to lessen the burden of this terrible disease on other families by setting up homes where caretakers can gather to receive love and support. Like many women, she gives all day, only to go home to give all night. Yet Leeza, like Barbara, gives so much of herself to others that she is too busy to realize the buildup behind her eyes. She told me that when she read this Wish on her BlackBerry after dropping her son off at school, she had to pull over and let herself cry. Sometimes all we need is a good cry and just a little love and we can keep going until the clouds fill up again and we need another letdown.

What I have learned from some of my friends whose children are grown and off on their own and whose parents have passed is how much they miss this stage in life and how quickly it all passes. They plead with me to enjoy every minute of it and tell me sad tales of an empty, lonely house. I try to remember this when I am feeling like an old stump, only good for sitting, but it is not always easy to talk yourself out of depletion. Sometimes a good cry clears my thoughts, or sometimes it is the love of a friend or the love of my husband. The best gratitude of all for the caretaker, however, is the sound of a child saying "Thank you." That does the trick.

"We ascend from a long and noble tradition of sisterhood; and the primitive need to bond, share, and get along to survive."

—BARBARA LAZAROFF

Words and Actions from Barbara

I have always believed that it is our duty as women, and as "sisters," to help our tribe—both less and more experienced, both strong and frail—stride the challenges of life's paths. There are so many pitfalls and mysteries in finding contentment, and although these women cannot live their lives vicariously and we cannot protect them (or ourselves) from all disasters, we can certainly instruct and offer alternatives to behaviors, actions, directions, words, and life patterns that are less than effective. We can attempt to provide a bit of a cushion for their falls, or a springboard for their advancements. It is natural and sensible, then, that historically many cultures have demonstrated women gathering together working communally for the good of all. They labored side by side raising, feeding, and protecting each other's children and the home site, as men went off to hunt. We ascend from a long and noble tradition of sisterhood; and the primitive need to bond, share, and get along to survive.

- *Think broadly; utilize one of your talents to help others. Can you paint, sing, play an instrument, or otherwise entertain someone or make them laugh or smile? Reflect on what abilities you have that can be a powerful tool to aid others.*

- *Can you cook, sew, or bake? Dance or draw? If so, teach a friend. I have a friend who is going to teach me how to knit.*

- *Are you skilled at accounting or good with technology? Perhaps you could help organize a friend's finances or documents, and then instruct them how to continue to do so themselves.*

- *Offer to fix a computer problem, or make a compilation of soothing music. Help paint a wall, or do a load of wash.*

- *Go over to a friend's home when she is too depressed to get out of bed, because you know that getting her up and out is vital. If she is physically ill, tidy up the home.*

- *Visit someone who has lost a loved one, not just in the first week or month, but well beyond when the reality of the loss is becoming cemented into this person's everyday life.*

- *Remind your friend: you must always believe in your ability to grow and learn, no matter how bleak the circumstances might seem.*

- *Ask her how you can specifically help her.*

"Call it a clan, call it
a network, call it a tribe, call it
a family: Whatever you call it,
whoever you are, you need one."

—JANE HOWARD, AUTHOR

"Well-behaved women
rarely make history."

—LAUREL THATCHER ULRICH, AUTHOR

"Create a history and legacy
you can be proud of; gather together,
do not deceive, do not yearn, but rather
earn your place of dignity. Speak truth,
engage in honest actions, change
what must be changed."

—BARBARA LAZAROFF

For You, I Wish

The Strength to Love

I want to wish you something, but I am too exhausted to tend to my own needs, much less the needs of others. I feel as if I am close to depletion in the absence of appreciation. I sit here with my pen, yet no words come to mind. Why, then, if I feel so drained, do I feel such a need to reach out and wish for you tonight? I have read that both the receiver and the giver of acts of kindness benefit equally. Maybe my needs are self-serving. I try hard to get to a place in my life where I give without expectations or needing anything in return. True giving must come un-conditionally.

Tonight, I relapse. Therefore, I look to nature, one of our greatest teachers. I wonder if the ocean ever says, "I don't want to make waves today or provide food and oxygen for the marine world." Does she tire? And the sun, does he ever complain about shining? No matter where you are, what continent, country, or town, if you are sitting on the beach or walking through a forest, the sun is there. He does not care if you are young or old, rich or poor, black or white. You do not even have to be ethical and he will still shine on you. As you look directly to the sun, you feel a direct relationship, a beam of heat and light connecting you to him. He makes you feel as if for that moment, you are the only living thing on this earth he is caring for. His warmth surrounds you and you forget that hundreds of miles away, a cornfield is being nourished by his giving, and another hundred miles away, a child in the ghetto is being warmed. That is how I want to love.

Tonight, when I seek love, I want the strength and goodness to love so that all those around me feel as if they are the only persons on this earth I love at that moment. I am tired and have little poetry for you, but I have a wish for you. I wish you all my love, and I wish you the strength to love all with all of your love. Some days it is all we have to give, and every day it is all we really need.

"I want the strength and goodness to love, so all those around me feel as if they are the only persons on this earth I love at that moment."

—TRICIA LaVOICE

✻ Reflection ✻

I considered removing this Wish from the mother collection because it was not very uplifting, so I wrote this reflection and set it aside. Then while in the process of finishing this book, I got a call from an old friend who is now a single parent trying to start her own business. She has no family nearby and works so hard at home that she rarely has time for friends. When she called, she was hysterical, feeling horrible as a mother who had no love to give her child and no patience to let him make mistakes. I asked her who loves her. Who rejuvenates her heart with love and support so she can love and support him—obviously no one? This Wish is raw and honest, but talks to the hearts of all mothers. If you are fortunate to have a strong support system, I salute you. If you are not, I cannot stress the need to build one. As the flight attendant always says, put your own oxygen mask on first before assisting others. And yes, as part of her support system, I did take her son for the weekend so she could rest. She would do the same for me, I am sure of that.

If there is a mother or caretaker out there who has not experienced the emotion of feeling nearly depleted and unappreciated, please write me and tell me your secret. Although many moments as a mother are full of love and appreciation, there are many times I find myself so tired I do not know where the strength will come from to continue with dinner, homework, and bedtime. On these nights, I go into robot mode, getting the job done without much emotion; and the little emotion I do have certainly does not lend itself to patience and kindness. My father would say, "Babies cry when they get tired, letting everyone around them know they need rest. While it is not socially acceptable for adults to start crying every time they feel tired, we still feel miserable like a baby needing a nap."

It would be wonderful if we could all love without expectations of being equally loved back, if we could give unconditionally, if we never got tired. But as the adults in the parent-child relationship, we are the givers, the providers, the ones with the open arms. Yet, we are humans and will make mistakes, tire, complain at times, indulge in self-pity, and simply want to be appreciated for our hard work. That is why when I wrote this Wish I was not wishing a mother the strength to love in order to benefit her family. I was really thinking about the mother herself, knowing if she had the strength to love, she would feel appreciated and rested. When I feel so worn out from life, longing to be loved and valued, I crave to love like the sun, to never tire, to be so filled with love I warm the hearts of people near and far, but that is not possible. When I am feeling tired and unappreciated, I have little to give the children, even less for my husband, and, certainly, nothing left for me.

These are the nights I long to check my inbox and find an encouraging e-mail waiting from a loving friend or two. Many times I find one with a friend checking in or someone asking about getting together. However, the nights I do not find an e-mail waiting I send one instead, believing this friend must need to feel loved, too. Interestingly, giving back to another caretaker can help lift one's spirits. It is reassuring just to read someone asking, "How are you?" I have found that this simple act of kindness replenishes the love temporarily absent from my heart, and I wish it to replenish the love from another loved one's exhausted soul, too.

As mothers and caretakers, we will tire, we will make mistakes, all of us, but if we are doing the best we can at that moment, we are doing just fine.

Words and Actions from Barbara

"I am so tired I cannot even see . . . yet I am too tired to fall asleep. I am thinking about how to resolve things, how to get my work done, help my boys, my parents."

These are my words from an e-mail I sent Tricia one night. How does this happen? As mothers, our job is never done and many times we find ourselves depleted. In these times, a friend can be a life saver. We must extend ourselves to each other to avoid getting too tired to enjoy our lives. A few suggestions for caring for your "mother friends":

- *Make or purchase dinner (preferably not fast food) for her family once a month, or you can rotate within a group of friends and each cook dinner one night a week thereby creating a "Cook Free" number of nights. You will benefit as well!*

- *Just say out loud, "I think you are a wonderful mother!" and "I am so proud to be your friend." You can also be specific about what you find admirable about her. You are so: creative, patient, kind, humorous, wise, and organized. I adore the quote "Women are great leaders, because we are always dealing with three children and two cookies!" We are the CEOs of our home, and some of us women are out in the workplace as well; we must help each other with the greatest and most important executive position in the world: raising healthy, productive, educated, and caring young adults. The environment and peace on this planet depends on the quality and character of our future generations. A dynamic child begins with a positive, well-intentioned, attentive mother.*

- *Give her a candle, some bubble bath and a peaceful CD. It will offer her a sense of calm.*

- *Surprise her and stop by with her favorite (healthy) snack, but if you find her at an inconvenient time, drop it off with a hug and leave.*

- *Help her rearrange furniture or plant in the garden or hang pictures or reorganize a cabinet.*

- *When she is going through a hard time, treat her to a casual dinner and a movie. If she loves the ocean or the mountains but rarely takes the time to enjoy them, drive her there so she can go for a walk, and relax and delight in the views. Ask a few friends to come along to share the experience.*

- *Use the mail to brighten her day. Keep mail supplies at your house to make it easy to just ship a simple token of love off with little effort. Mail her favorite candy (or something healthier!) or a box of tea bags with a note saying, "Sharing a moment with you, remember I am there in spirit."*

- *If you can afford it, send her for a massage; perhaps the tribe can all contribute. You might try to do the massage yourself. (One of my dearest friends was hospitalized and we all took turns massaging her feet! Some of us had more natural talent than others, but we were all appreciated.)*

- *Once when I was not feeling well I had a "mother-friend" who came to my home every evening for a week walk my dogs and close up the house for the night. In return, I took her children for the weekend and she and her husband had some much-needed time alone. There are countless ways for mothers to support one another.*

"The house does not rest upon
the ground, but upon a woman."

—MEXICAN PROVERB

"Sometimes I feel I cannot find another ounce of strength to do any more that day until I look at one of my sons, or see a dear friend's face. When they smile, cry, or ask for help, I unearth the strength. As "sisters," and as mothers, we are the wellsprings of the family and the community; we must remember to shower each other with care, to replenish our own essence."

—BARBARA LAZAROFF

For You, I Wish

The Chance to Observe Like an Art Student

I observed like a student of art devouring a museum piece as he brought you the loveliest of his paintings, but you sent him away, demanding more. He entered again holding his best work, his shoulders broad, his smile long, but the measuring stick you held was gauged for others and he fell short. With his head hung low, he promised greatness and returned to his work. I saw delight in your eyes, heard you boasting of his talent as you felt sure your frustration pushed him to his best. Again he entered, this time a bit unsure; you saw excellence yet asked for perfection. Then and there, I observed like a student of art devouring a museum piece, his epiphany that he would never be enough in your eyes, never live up to your expectations, so in survival mode, he held his shoulders broad, his smile long, and returned to his work, never needing your approval again. For you, I wish the chance to observe like a student of art devouring a museum piece.

"Our intentions lose their meaning if our children's interpretations are different from what we are trying to convey."

—Tricia LaVoice

✳ Reflection ✳

I was asked to write this Wish by a friend of mine who was very upset about the relationship her son had with his father, her ex-husband. She said her son confided in her that he never felt he was good enough in his father's eyes and that no matter what he did, his father found fault with him. My friend was concerned that this was affecting her son's self-esteem, and she was very frustrated. She asked me to write something she could share with the father to hopefully open his eyes. As is often the case with writing, I had to put the thought on the back burner until the Wish came to me. But as I wrote it, I felt I was being somewhat unfair. I knew this father well, and I knew that he loved his son very much. I knew he was very proud of his boy, and many times he had told me great things about his son. I also knew the father thought he was doing his son right by pushing him, and he believed it is a father's responsibility to prepare his son for the world. My friend was grateful for the Wish, but she never gave it to her ex-husband. I was glad about that.

I think about all of us parents and the way we see ourselves versus the way our children see us. Just recently, my daughter Olivia saw a Wish I wrote on the home page of our local yoga studio. After reading it, she looked to me and said, "Wow, Mom, that was good, but I would think you would be a nicer person if you wrote stuff like that." I guess I took it as a compliment.

I believe that in our hearts we are doing our best for our children. I do, however, think we all need to reflect every once in a while and look at our parenting style through the eyes of our children. Are we complaining too much? Are we sufficient in celebrating their achievements? Are we harping on their failures? Have we truly given thought to what we really want for our children—for them to like themselves, for them to feel confident—and are we helping them execute these goals?

All of us, including myself, could read this Wish and fail to spot ourselves in it. After speaking to her ex-husband about their son, my friend said she thought it was pointless to send the Wish. Her ex-husband saw her as being too lenient, and he felt just as strongly about the damage this leniency was doing to their son. Obviously, she disagreed with him. In my marriage, I know there are times when I feel that Rich and I are coming from two totally different points of view with the kids, and neither one of us is very open to seeing the other parent's viewpoint. Self-reflecting and recognizing our faults is difficult, but when it comes to the sensitive subject of parenting, it can be almost impossible. The issue here, though, is our children and how they see us as parents. Going to the source and having honest conversations with our children, allowing them to feel safe to speak their minds, may be the best way to truly understand the effects of our parenting. Ultimately, our intentions lose their meaning if our children's interpretations are different from what we are trying to convey.

Words and Actions from Barbara

There are many ways to help our children develop a positive self-image; we must start by having healthy self-images as parents. Our children will look to us for signals regarding how we relate to the world around us, how we cope, what we determine to be a healthy, successful, happy life. Hopefully these are authentic values, not merely forms of "success" measured in fame or monetary gain alone.

In our quest to guide our children, we must be careful not to project our expectations and hopes onto them for our own satisfaction or self-aggrandizing purposes. Perhaps the family business is medicine, or in my case, design and the restaurant industry; I cannot expect my sons to follow in the family businesses. If they wish to do so, I will vigorously support them. However, my true hope is that they fulfill their own personal destiny. As parents we must be firm about good work/study habits and character, however, we must refrain from excessively criticizing our children—forcing their life and career decisions to parallel ours—and remember to constantly show love and support.

- *Focus on the positive, and highlight your children's strengths.*

- *Work on improving their mastery in areas in which they are less accomplished. Practice reading, throwing a ball, swimming, biking, mathematics, or art with them. Ask them what they would like help with. If you find you have conflicts when you try to teach your child, you might consider hiring a tutor, if you can afford one; if you cannot, ask the child's school for additional help. There are also superb after-school athletic programs, volunteer tutors, and community centers with a variety of programs that help cultivate proficiency in a broad range of areas.*

- *Make an encouraging poster or plaque by hand and hang it in their room or outside their bedroom door. I am a great believer in the influence of inspiring quotes.*

- *Randomly text your children a message of pure love and encouragement.*

- *Invite them to your room and ask them to sit down. Tell them how proud you are of them.*

- *Tell your child, "You do not have to be the very best at everything you aspire to at this moment, but if you strive to be better, you will reach one or more of your goals and find deep satisfaction knowing your efforts were realized."*

- *Reward them for effort, not just accomplishment. We should always remember the fable of the tortoise and the hare: the hare was far too sure of himself and got lazy; he figured he did not need to keep a consistent pace, he could stop and catch up later, but the tortoise kept moving diligently along, and to everyone's astonishment beat the naturally speedy hare. However, if the tortoise hadn't won he still would have been a star as far as I'm concerned; I would recognize his faith in himself, his tenacity, his courage, and the sheer magnitude of his resolute effort.*

- *Pay attention to your speech. If you want to point out a behavior that requires adjusting, first express at least two things you feel your children have done that are positive. Wait a few minutes, and let them enjoy the praise. Perhaps give them a hug. Then bring up the behavior you think they can improve on.*

- *Talk to your children about things that you needed to improve upon when you were young. Tell them how you felt when you failed at something. Reinforce what you discovered about yourself from those missteps or disappointments, what you did to gain proficiency in those areas, and how those lessons have guided you, preventing you from repeating your mistakes.*

"Life is a grand canvas and you should
throw all the paint on it that you can."

—DANNY KAYE, ACTOR, DANCER, SINGER,
AND ACCOMPLISHED AMATEUR CHEF

"Be brave, be observant, be adventurous, be exuberant, be tenacious, be curious. Ask questions, lots of questions. Find as many answers as you can. Sometimes there is more than one answer to the same question; sometimes those answers can change. The more you explore, the more you will discover, about the world and about yourself. Be a student, become a teacher, maintain an unfettered mind, and you will remain a scholar of life forever."

—BARBARA LAZAROFF

For You, I Wish

The Boy on the Couch

I rushed from my bedroom to the kitchen, with a million things to do. The corner of my eye caught a young boy sitting alone on the edge of the couch. I quickly called out to him, "You good?"

"I'm good."

I went about my chaos as if averting the end of the world by returning all phone calls, paying the bills, and picking up the laundry. I moved like a tire across a trail; the faster I spun, the less I caught in my treads. The boy the universe entrusted me to guide and nurture called out from the couch, "Mom, you good?"

I ask myself, "How long does it take to make a memory? How long does it take to make a difference? Three hours a day? One hour a day? Ten minutes here and there?" It's just a small thing that I remember about that day.

Think of your memories. I loved the trips to the shore, the nights out at the movies. However, my favorite memories are the ones ten minutes here and there, the walks around the block with my father, the quick cups of tea with my mother, listening to my big sister's stories about her day. These are the moments that molded my thoughts, instilled my values, tended to my self-worth. Remarkable that the right ten minutes can stay with us forever, making a lifetime memory. We cannot be expected to notice every new freckle dance across this boy's face, but ten simple minutes, the right minutes, can make a memory.

I flew through the kitchen again, this time slower in pace, but my mind still raced. Then the realization that the world was not ending hit my brakes and stopped me in my tracks. I walked into the family room and looked at the kindness in my son's eyes, I felt the warmth of his hand as I took it in mine and I relished in the delight on his face when I said, "Come, let's take a few minutes and go outside to watch the world change."

For you, I wish a memory as sweet as that of the boy on the couch.

"How long does it take to make a memory? How long does it take to make a difference? Remarkable that the right ten minutes can stay with us forever, making a lifetime memory."

—TRICIA LaVOICE

❋ Reflection ❋

I was pregnant with our fourth child when Rich and I were at a dinner party with some of the parents from Olivia's school. The woman hosting the party had two children herself, but came from a family of four. I remember so clearly her telling me that she felt she never received enough attention growing up and she hoped that by having two children herself, she would have the time and energy to give each child plenty of individual attention. I rubbed my big, bulging belly, feeling life move inside me, thinking, "What have I done? Can I be enough for each of them?" Then she offered me hope. She told me how her mother would make an effort each night to lie down with each one of her children in their beds to make sure they all got alone mommy time each day. I thought, "Yes, I can do that."

Bills and responsibilities are a reality. We all have limited time for leisure, and I imagine we all wish we had more time and energy for our children. It is unfair to assume one mother has more time for her children versus another, based solely on the number of children she has. A mother of one can be less involved in her child's life than a mother of six. It all depends on the time and energy given. That is when the beauty of creativity comes into play. With just a little thought, we can turn everyday events into meaningful memories; with a little effort, we can make our children's worlds that much more beautiful to reflect upon.

There was another mother of four at our school whom I would watch interact with her children from time to time. On field day, I would watch her as she walked with her daughter from one event to the next, as the rest of us moms hung together, chatting. She was creating a memory, knowing how happy her daughter was to have her mother's undivided attention as she competed in her events.

It is so important to give our children beautiful, meaningful memories from their childhoods because the time we take to make them is what helps define our children, building on their self-worth. My father used to say, "No child asks to be born. So true, but how easy it is to get caught up in the hustle and bustle of life and forget to stop and make memories."

We did not have a lot of money growing up, but we had enough for a middle-class American family to enjoy life. We took a yearly vacation to an island and had our weekly horseback riding lessons. I had a pretty Easter dress to wear each year and plenty of toys under the tree. However, what I remember most is lying on the couch at night watching television with my mother, and the way she would scratch my scalp. I hated the weird noise it made inside my head, but I loved lying in her arms, so I never complained. I remember how she would let me in her room on Saturday nights and how I would watch her get ready to go out with my father for the night. She would play Dionne Warwick music and ask me how she looked while I danced in the mirror. Of course, there was not a more beautiful woman in the world to me. When she was gone, it was okay, I had my time, I had my memory. The little things that we make special, the things that do not take much time, just a little effort, can make all the difference in our children's lives.

"Can I be enough for each of them?"

— TRICIA LAVOICE

Words and Actions from Barbara

The sweetest memories don't require anything but a little time, thought, creativity, and sometimes a childlike sense of fun!

- *While driving, play "Race the Moon." Watch how the moon follows you home, sometimes appearing way in the lead, and then falling far behind with a turn in the road. Also, while driving, have your kids close their eyes and try to guess where you are situated at that moment, or if they don't know the destination, ask them to guess where you are both going.*

- *Let each child pick what is served for dinner once a week.*

- *Go out on a "date" once a month, or more often, with each child separately. Perhaps a movie, dinner, a museum, the zoo, a planetarium, an aquarium, a sports event. Ask your children where they would like to go.*

- *During dinner, play "Who Is Coming to Dinner?" Each family member gets to "invite" three people to the meal and must explain their selection: famous or not famous, from the past or present, real or fictional. (Assume all loved ones are already included.) As an added novelty, you can discuss whether your guests would approve of the food being served!*

- *Push the furniture back and have a family picnic somewhere in the house.*

- *Have a family sleepover party in the TV room. Roll out the sleeping bags or put the throw pillows out. Play board games, charades, get a karaoke machine, and be silly!*

- *Make one night a week movie night and have the family sit together and watch a film. Have the children help you make popcorn and healthy snacks. Afterward, that evening, or the next, discuss the film.*

- *Read books out loud—those that capture the attention of all the kids.*

- *Burn a CD of your kids favorite music and share it with them while you drive. Sing along if they are agreeable to the idea.*

- *If you have a home office, or projects you have brought home, have your kids sit on the floor or across the desk from you. Tell them they are your co-workers today. Pretending to be at work with your children empowers them and fosters confidence. You can put a time frame on this if you need to concentrate. Give your kids a task like sharpening pencils, faxing, and helping to copy information. Let them feel like they are increasing your productivity. Compliment them, even if their presence causes little delays. When my older son Cameron was only six, he started to sit at my drafting table and draw plans of an imaginary project, "The Most Perfect Restaurant Design in the World," and "My Dream House," which happily looked a lot like ours except one room was made completely out of pizza. (I have saved these because they are priceless!) My biggest concern was making certain he did not fall off the drafting chair!*

- *Look at family photos and create a scrapbook together for someone else in the family.*

- *Go together and pick out seeds and then plant them. Watch how $1.99 can miraculously grow into something beautiful to smell or eat. Show a child how a potato can sprout, or how an artichoke can produce a truly unusual flower.*

- *On the internet, or in the library, you will find fascinating and easy home science projects: Make a tornado in a bottle, a functioning potato or orange clock, or demonstrate how water and oil don't mix; explain the concept of density. Pour food dye into a vase with a flower and watch as the color rises up the stem and alters the color of the flower petals; then explain how plants get their nourishment. Experiments with magnets, gravity, light, and many more will fascinate your child. Depending on your kids' ages, you can simplify the explanations or expand upon them. You will educate, as well as delight, your children, as you share unforgettable moments together.*

- *For younger children, make masks or costumes out of items already in the home. You can use shoe boxes, ribbons, and old sheets, pots for hats, tin foil, old clothes, newspapers, and magazines. You can also create collages on paper, frames, or serving trays; dioramas; window décor (paper snowflakes are a classic favorite of mine); mobiles; and welcome signs for the front door. Musical instruments are easy to create with rice, nuts, Lego pieces, or other metal or plastic objects inside plastic containers or a metal thermos; they make terrific shakers; or you can give your child a metal, plastic or wood spoon. They will marvel at how the sounds change with the different materials. (Take care to never leave small objects around children who might swallow them; therefore, use common sense when allowing your children to select the objects they place in their "instruments," especially if they have younger siblings.)*

- *Prepare your child for a bubble bath with soothing music. Use battery-operated candles for safety, unless you are present and the flame candles are not in reaching distance. This is a terrific way to provide your kids with some relaxation time, particularly if they have trouble sleeping. Never leave young children alone in the bath: safety first! Privacy is for older adolescents and young teens.*

For You, I Wish

A River's Love

All the river knows is to journey home, letting nothing stand in her way. In times of drought, she flows with calmness, low to the ground, not rousing the earth. In times of surge, she roars, rapidly racing her course. Place an obstacle in her way and she will overcome it with her determination and spirit—squeezing under, over, and around the largest of boulders, the smallest of debris. All she knows is to journey home.

All I know is to love you, letting nothing stand in my way. In times of struggle, I will remain gentle, providing you clarity. In times of conflict, I will move swiftly, softening your ache. If you detach from me, I will tenderly wait. If you place an obstacle in my way, I will trounce it; and if you find resentment and fury within me, I will humble myself. All the river knows is to journey home, as all I know is to love you. For you, I wish a river's love.

"All the river knows is to journey home,
as all I know is to love you."

—Tricia LaVoice

❋ Reflection ❋

The greatest gift we can offer our children is to love them uncon-
ditionally. It is the essential ingredient that allows them to grow and
experience love with others throughout their lives. When children feel
unconditional love, they learn to love themselves, to have loving friends,
and to be loving friends themselves. It is the building block, stable and
healthy, that allows them to be in loving relationships as adults and
become loving parents.

It is important that we do not take for granted the terms of uncon-
ditional love, and that we verbally express it. Many children will not
understand that they are loved unconditionally and will focus on their
parents' expectations of good grades, achievements in sports, and proper
behavior. As parents, of course we want our children to achieve and to be
happy, but we know we will love them just as much if they fail. We also
understand that if one of our children struggles while the other achieves,
this also does not affect how much we love our children. However, young
minds are sensitive. It is important to explain to a child what uncondi-
tional love is and how you have loved him or her that way from the start
and will until the end, no matter what happens along the way.

I have always told my children that I may not always like their
behavior, but I always love them. Of course, as a mother of four, each
one of my children has asked at one point or another which one of them
I love the most, and my answer is always the same: Nature makes it
impossible for me to love one of you more. As a mother, I am given an
endless ability to love you all equally and without conditions. This usu-
ally quiets them for a while.

I have also found that as my children grow older and the teenage
years begin to take over our home, there are fewer and fewer opportu-
nities to express my unconditional love to them. However, it is just as
important to remind them of this love in these difficult years as it ever
was. Many times, when one of them is acting like a classic teenager and
fighting me on an issue for no apparent reason other than to argue, I
have found that if I can muster the strength to throw out an "I love you"
and "I only want the best for you" (when what I really want to do is send

them to live with an aunt), they calm down more quickly and hear me rather than fight me.

Loving a child unconditionally is a blessing for both the child and the parent. I cannot think of anything more rewarding than a life filled with loving memories with your children. Barbara's mother, Ellie, is a beautiful example of a mom dedicated to her children from the start to the end. She has maternal energy that is felt by all in her life. I love listening to her yell to Barbara as she walks out the door to be careful driving or when Barbara is sick, Ellie worries for her as if she were still her little girl. At 84, Ellie tells me all the time, "You never stop being a mother, Trish, but they grow so fast, so make sure you hug them and tell them every day how much you love them."

I really try to live by her words, hoping to have similar beautiful memories to hold when I am 84. However, what is much more important is that my children hold memories of being unconditionally loved when <u>they</u> are 84.

"We strive to give our children a feeling of their place in the world by grounding them with home and family—a heritage of belonging. If we have done a fine job, one day they will soar off and find a place of belonging wherever life may take them, because they carry 'home' in their heart."

—BARBARA LAZAROFF

A tenet that has become truer as I have grown more intuitive and aware:

"I've learned that people will forget what you said, people will forget what you did, but people will never forget how you made them feel."

—MAYA ANGELOU, POET AND AUTHOR

Words and Actions from Barbara

As a mother, the most salient legacy you can imprint upon your children is the irreplaceable and powerful gift of acceptance and support—purely for being the people they are. Your "gift" of genuine and unconditional love possesses a matchless value. These are the memories that will carry them through their lives. Your love will have a far greater impact on your children than any video game or pair of shoes they once swore they could not live without.

- *If they are out of line, always tell your children you are disapproving of their behavior, not them.*

- *While they are out with friends, send them a loving text.*

- *Randomly and often tell them, "I love you."*

- *Put notes in their lunch boxes. Be respectful of their privacy as they get older.*

- *Hug them. Physical affection is an important emotional connection.*

- *If, in moments of anger or frustration, your child says mean things to you, refrain from saying unkind things back to them. You can tell them that their words are hurtful and disrespectful, but do not mirror their immature and rude behavior. Remember, you are an adult.*

- *Turn off your cell phone when you spend time with them. This lets them know you do not want to be disturbed because they are the most important people in your life.*

- *Frame their artwork and achievements and hang them on the wall, or tape them up on the refrigerator. Acknowledge their work more than once. Say, "Every time I look at your art I feel happy" or "You should be so proud of your report card, and I love looking at it every day, because I know you had to work very hard to achieve these grades." Their grades do not have to be stellar for you to say this earnestly if they have tried their best.*

- *On cold mornings, throw their clothes in the dryer for a few minutes to warm them up. Preheat the car before they come out to go to school.*
- *Walk in the rain together.*

For You, I Wish

The Lessons of Boyhood

So the day has come when they call you a man, when all you have known is to be a boy. So how do you know how to be a man? By remembering everything you learned being a boy. If one person on the team breaks the rules, the game is ruined for the whole team. The go-cart you built in your garage with your best friend is a much sweeter ride than any you can buy at the store. The only time you should be in a box is when you are rolling down a hill.

Climb the corporate ladder like you climbed a tree, never looking back or letting fear get in your way while avoiding the sap. Remember what you learned being a boy. Things that make your heart pound are worth doing twice. If it smells bad, it probably is bad. The best place to find safety in times of trouble is in a pair of arms. And like a game of tennis, it is better to serve than to be served. Life will flash like a summer vacation: get to the beach, find love in a book, and visit with friends. Never forget what you learned being a boy when becoming a man, remembering the most important lesson of all: your legs will carry you on your journey, but your family will carry you on their backs.

For you, I wish the lessons of boyhood.

"Raising children who are compassionate and giving happens when we begin instilling altruistic behavior early—not by words alone, but by example and clear and consistent actions."

—BARBARA LAZAROFF

"The understanding of atomic physics is child's play, compared with the understanding of child's play."

—DAVID KRESH, POET

Like many friends, Barbara and I became friends when our sons,
Byron and Billy, became friends. Billy spent a lot of time over at
Barbara's home, as Byron spent a lot of time at our home. Byron
just slipped into place, as one of our own when he was at the house.
I wrote this Wish for Byron as he turned the wonderful age of thirteen.
Fittingly, Barbara writes the reflection and actions to follow.

Enjoy, Tricia

Words and Actions from Barbara

As parents we are shaping the future of our country and the
world; children are the next generation of leaders, voters, citizens,
teachers, entrepreneurs, and "architects" of not only buildings,
but also institutions, medicine, law, culture, and social change.

Childhood should be a time of joy and adventure, but equally
a journey of growth. Youth is a time of learning to share, to co-
operate, to compete, to communicate, and to accept that sometimes we win and other times we lose. Disappointments are an
opportunity to become stronger and more diligent in our efforts
and our relationships. We want our children to recall a childhood
filled with happy moments, while structuring their developmen-
tal years through adulthood with lessons in responsibility, organization, altruism, good family values, as well as instruction in good
citizenship. These lessons needn't always be somber and tedious;
there are creative and joyful ideas for guiding our children to be
the best they can be!

As I was writing my thoughts on what I believe creates a well-
rounded and healthy young person, I started to realize that many
of the virtues and character qualities are the very values that my
mom taught me. Not surprisingly, they also echoed in the guidelines I was asked to adhere to as a Camp Fire Girl, a Brownie, and a
Girl Scout. I then reread the Boy Scouts of America Oath, and these
principles are indeed ones that we should hope our children, and

we as adults, aspire to and work toward. We learn many of these lessons by watching the behavior of those around us, primarily our parents, if they are involved, loving, and compassionate people. How we respond and cope with our triumphs and failures are often a reflection of how we have seen those we respect and love respond to these situations.

Although as parents we often feel that our words should carry authority and profound meaning, it is more often our actions that speak the loudest. Our children watch how we treat those around us—from our spouses, and other family members such as our elderly parents, to people who provide us with services such as those individuals who bag our groceries, or the attendant at the gas station and the busboy in the diner. They are aware at the youngest of ages how we interact with figures of authority such as police officers and teachers. They hear and see how we behave in a traffic jam—do we yell or use profane language? Are we curt, impatient, demanding, or demeaning of the salespeople in a department store? All these are lessons our child assimilates on a very primal level. We can produce respectful, kind-hearted, altruistic children, or those who feel entitled, superior to those around them, and who will grow up to treat others with arrogance and disdain.

Egotism is a disastrous blueprint for forming healthy, happy relationships that are genuine and well balanced. Individuals who lack consideration for others often form relationships based on superficial concepts such as material acquisitions or status—whatever advances their personal goals. An indulged, haughty, undisciplined child can also develop contempt for authority; this arrogance can lead to individuals who feel they are "above the law." We see a breakdown of marriage through adultery and poor communication; and we have witnessed the extreme illegal and immoral behavior in public arenas, most recently our financial systems and the growing scandals in our religious sectors. The increasing number of divorces, lawsuits, and incarcerations, as well as the outrageous public institution scams, is an indication that our interpersonal exchanges, communities, and civil and financial institutions require more intervention at a far earlier crossroad.

The recent destruction of many people's lives who trusted "leaders of society," icons who were actually self-important and lacking true virtue, is indicative of many of these societal shortcomings. Honor, respect, morality, loyalty, and the courage to speak out against injustice are all values that are instilled very early on and honed throughout life. Perhaps we would see far less exploitation in the world arena if there were more compassionate, involved, and yes, disciplined guiding figures, role models, and social systems in everyone's upbringing.

Certainly, in time, our children start emulating their peers; therefore, our attention to their friendships is essential. Our most important job as parents is to instill in our kids character, self-confidence, a sense of community, purpose, compassion, a love of education and a desire to live a life of purpose and value. How do we accomplish such a heady task and still raise a child with joy and cherished memories? If we are a consistent presence in their young lives, we have a better hope of producing young adults who have a strong sense of personal esteem and a powerful connection to family so that outside influences such as drugs, drinking, promiscuity, or simply poor work habits and rude behavior do not influence them as they do with children who feel less attached to family values.

We do the best we can, knowing we will make mistakes. Divorce, an absent father or mother, economic stresses, or health issues can all impact our efforts. It is essential to realize that we all meet with life's disappointments, and that rather than try to protect our children from every stumble, these moments build character and can create situations wherein they learn to face obstacles and develop techniques for problem solving—lessons they will need throughout life.

Additionally, providing parameters of proper behavior toward other individuals, animals, and our environment are all paramount in the evolution of raising well-adjusted world citizens. Also important is showing respect to all people, honoring differences, caring for our earth's creatures, and taking care of personal property—their own as well as others'. This instills young people with a deep appreciation for their own bodies and minds, and the rights of others. These considerations are all essential aspects of maturity. Profound understanding of the balance of our place in the world in relation to others, and how to draw the lines between our rights and the rights of others is a complex and sometimes lifelong series of lessons. My boys' school had a wonderful poster hanging in the halls. It said: "My rights end where yours begin."

Our balancing act as conscientious parents is to provide our children with both love and responsibilities—a playground of imagination mingled with a program of chores. This formula facilitates a more confident roadmap to young adulthood. It takes much more work as an involved parent to read with our children, make certain they are reading, check their homework, consult with their teachers, be aware of what they are looking at on the computer and watching on television, truly knowing their friends and their buddies' parents, knowing where they go when they leave the house, and what they are doing. These practices can certainly be exhausting, but it is what constitutes good parenting.

Try to do as much as you can—that alone is a good beginning. It is far more effective to be involved than to just hope your kids are behaving, getting their work done, and being good citizens. If you do not provide a groundwork of good work/study habits and discipline in childhood, don't expect that it will be easy to instill these traits much later on. The most important step in building a strong house is the foundation. Get that right, spend the time and effort at the ground level, and the walls have a better chance of going up straight and enduring the storms of life.

- *Read to your children every day; promote the importance of reading, and make it fun. (I used to dress up as various characters, change voices, act out the books, and ask the kids to do certain parts.) Reading underscores the importance of education and is one of the most important tools for excelling in school. Education is the vehicle for a life of choice with regard to work and fulfilling dreams.*

- *Storytelling is a wonderful way for a pre-reader to "read" to you! My sons and I had a couple of characters around which we would create stories. I would tell the first one, and they would tell the next one every night. This practice also teaches your children the fine art of listening, a skill even adults need to constantly enhance.*

  As your children get older and are reading more sophisticated work that requires analysis of characters, plot, or writing techniques, it is helpful to read the material as well and discuss it with them. You could also form a parent-child book club, or have a friend who is knowledgeable in literature guide them. Children sometimes have fascinating personal interpretations of a literature selection—some brilliantly perceptive, others decidedly off course and in need of encouraging redirection. Another suggestion: as a child, my mom always required that we have a dictionary next to us while reading. She also created a contest to see who could learn the most new vocabulary words that week. We would find interesting new words and construct sentences with them every day. We made certain that some of the results were quite amusing!

- *As your children develop, if they resist reading in their spare moments, as mine did at times, you may have to implement a barter system: an hour of computer time or video play in exchange for an hour of reading.*

- *Reinforce the concept that after your children graduate, continuing to educate themselves is an important practice that will enrich their lives; reading, formal classes, or online studies are all excellent methods. I have a girlfriend who took an Art History class and an Italian class with her grown son. Whatever field you are in, you can always learn more.*

- *Display words of inspiration and guidance in your children's rooms, or place them in their lunchboxes every day. As your children mature, they may want this practice to remain at home!*

- *I think every parent and child should read "IF" by Rudyard Kipling. This poem was read at my son's Bar Mitzvah. You can adjust it to relate to a girl as well. Each line is a gem, speaking to the virtues of patience, honor, perseverance, dignity, honesty, forgiveness, humility, and so on.*

> *"If you can keep your head when all about you,*
> *Are losing theirs and blaming it on you;*
> *If you can trust yourself when all men doubt you,"*

The poem also directs us to transcend lies and hatred; to stand nobly with kings and compassionately with the common man. It speaks of aspiration as the mere catalyst toward achieving your goal.

> *"If you can dream—and not make dreams your master;*
> *If you can think—and not make thoughts your aim."*

As well as learning to cope with both success and failure, appreciate that both have more in common than we realize. Living with humility, not false pride about our good fortune is important, and alternatively not succumbing to complete devastation when challenged by great adversity. This tempered perspective is the key to a life of equilibrium and the mark of a man (or a woman) of distinctive character.

> *"If you can meet with Triumph and Disaster*
> *And treat those two imposters just the same."*

The poem celebrates an individual who can bear witness to his life's work being destroyed, and gather the strength to rebuild again. A person who respects people, but is not unduly impressed by anyone; a man of both daring and quiet dignity. The final lines sum up with the sage advice of filling every minute of your existence with purpose, and giving life everything you have within you, fully understanding that each minute is finite, and when it passes it is gone forever. The aspects of character referred to in *"IF"* are poetic guideposts for the making of a boy into a man.

> *"If you can fill the unforgiving minute*
> *With sixty seconds' worth of distance run,*
> *Yours is the Earth and everything that's in it,*
> *And which is more; you'll be a Man, my son!"*

Not surprisingly, the Boy Scouts of America's Oath highlights adherence to similar virtues: They are trustworthiness, loyalty, helpfulness, friendliness, courtesy, kindness, obedience, cheerfulness, thriftiness, bravery, cleanliness, and reverence. The motto of being prepared and the slogan to do a good deed every day are habits and actions we should all work toward.

- *Whether your child is a member of the Scouts, or a different club or organization, the Oath is a terrific guideline to post!*

- *Have your children write one quote, dream, or aspiration that they have read or created. Have them keep a journal or post them on a board! Perhaps not just in their room . . . maybe everyone could take a turn to post the best quote of the day on the refrigerator or an official "Idea Board."*

- *There are many excellent books about raising responsible children. Read them; and discuss them with friends, your parents, and counselors.*

- *Instruct your children that every time they meet someone to address them directly, shake hands, and look the person in the eye when speaking to them. This is a behavior I stressed very early on with my boys; it has served them well when meeting people in both private and public situations. It is a sign of respect toward the individual and exudes personal confidence. This behavior teaches your child to be in the moment and to acknowledge everyone with dignity and kindness.*

- *Join a parent support group; seek guidance if you feel you need advice—we all do at times. If you do not have family or friends nearby, you may have to find other people to guide you.*

- *If your children are still fortunate to have grandparents, incorporate them as fully as you are able into your nurturing and educational mission. Discuss your family rules and expectations regarding food, TV, and computer-viewing guidelines, chores, bedtime, disciplinary styles, and any other core issues. If you, your folks, and your in-laws can agree on these general terms, engage them as your most responsible and loving helpmates (understanding that grandparents deserve a little bit of relaxation with regard to what they enforce—they've earned it)! Children may heed advice from a grandparent more easily than from their mom or dad—especially if the subject is an issue of conflict concerning a parent. For example, my dad is a very amusing man; he has a truly silly sense of humor and can often defuse a stressful situation. My mom is always telling my boys, "I don't just love you, I like you, too!"*

- *Her warmth can often persuade them to be a little easier on me! My boys are also very keen on making their grandparents proud of them, and they try to act accordingly. Involving grandparents teaches children the importance of respecting their elders and valuing the knowledge gained from experience.*

  Whether your parents are musicians, homemakers, doctors, mechanics, gardeners, pilots, military personnel, salespeople, chefs, architects, or taxi cab drivers, each parent has pragmatic knowledge and messages to share. Grandparents instruct their grandchildren in the history of our times and their family narrative. If they are healthy and willing, and have some time to devote to their grandchildren, they make the most exuberant fans at school games; and are patient bedtime readers, math tutors, ball-throwers, movie companions, card or chess opponents, baking or knitting teachers, and truly wonderful listeners!

Grandmothers and grandfathers fulfill myriad other delightful roles—most important, providing unconditional love. They are such fun, always delighted to see their brilliant, talented, gorgeous grandchildren!

- *If you are aware of a child that could use some adult companionship, a Big Brother or Big Sister organization is something you can suggest to the busy mom or dad (if the dad is not in the home, often boys would do well to have a Big Brother or a male role model such as an uncle or family friend). My boys do not have a father in the home, and I think having male tutors for them was a good choice. A friend had done this with her boys and I thought it was a terrific idea. Often after completing their work, the guys would go out and throw a ball around, play music, or simply talk. Now there is a man in my life who relates to them and rides a bike, takes them shooting at a range, and taught one son to weld and the other to fish, but I still employ a male tutor when we need one.*

- *You children's choice of friends matters greatly, and having communicative relationships with their parents is important. Work on that, have them over, or bring a cake or fruit basket and tell them you would like to visit and just get to know each other.*

- *Some parents are far more interested in the social and economic standing of their children's friends; however, sharing similar parenting styles and values is far more important. Learn to be both firm and flexible; you need to constantly reconsider your parenting style as your child develops and becomes more responsible.*

Communicate with the other parents; your child may tell you, "So-and-so's parents say it is okay!" Have parent-child get-together-style play-dates; you will discover a great deal about how the other parents interact with their children, and then discuss your expectations and theirs with regard to behavior. Factors such as family rules, moral expectations, and education and study styles should matter to you far more than the race, religion, or ethnic backgrounds of your children's friends. Your child will be part of a global experience when they mature; therefore, as they learn to accept and respect other people's customs, their development as kind, intelligent, and well-functioning world citizens will be broader and more refined.

- *If you can afford it, travel! It is so vital in educating your children, particularly if you live in a very homogenous area. The times my children traveled not only abroad, but within the U.S., have greatly furthered their understanding of how other people live and think. If you have limited resources, explore the parts of your city your child has not visited. Some children never see other areas of their own city, so discover them with your child, bring a group of parents and children, and discuss the cultural diversity. The children can make drawings or shoebox dioramas of what impressed or surprised them the most.*

- *If you cannot travel, and your hometown offers little diversity, then books, movies, videos, and some television specials can expand your child's knowledge of the world. There are also children's museums, and school and library programs that address issues such as racial and ethnic differences and traditions. Children who live in urban areas with a variety of cultures that have not assimilated well may experience cultural and racial tensions. These programs can provide a platform for discovery and discussion for both children (who tend to be more open) and adults (who sometimes negatively influence their children due to their own prejudices).*

  Involve your child in a sport; this can be a terrific character-building activity. Children gain confidence as they become more proficient in a chosen sport, learning important life lessons and often forging friendships that last a lifetime. The process will highlight the importance of self-confidence and personal motivation in individual sport, and the significance of strategic teamwork in group activities. These traits and skills transfer well to work study/ habits, and later to the business world. Both individual sport and team involvement stress the value of tenacity through vigorous practice, the importance of constant and clear communication, the necessity to accept direction, and as in many life situations, the necessity to gracefully cope with both victory and defeat.

Many of these lessons will be lost on your child if the sport is challenging but not entertaining. Don't compel your children to engage in a particular sport based on your personal passion, or your neighbor's; they will be far more motivated to play if they have an authentic interest in the sport. The other most significant factor influencing the sport's impact on instilling superior virtues such as sportsmanship and responsibility is the character of the coach. This is the most influential person on the team, and he or she will be a significant part of your child's life for many hours of the day. Get to know this person; if he or she is firm about good conduct and maintains a zero-tolerance rule for berating teammates, opponents, and arguing with officials, your child-athlete will acquire positive life experiences. The coach will also teach your child that there are negative consequences for poor sportsmanship, rude or abusive behavior, antagonistic or arrogant "star" attitude, lack of genuine effort, being late to a practice or game, or not showing up at all—life lessons many employers wish some of their staff had learned in youth.

Remember to be supportive of your child, but reinforce the coach's decisions as well. If you disagree with the coach, discuss the issue privately. Just as you are the authority figure in your home, the coach is the executive in his or her arena. If you are qualified, consider contributing to your child-athlete's team by assistant coaching. You can also support the team by bringing refreshments, offering to photograph or video the games, or carpooling some of the team members to and from the games. The more you encourage, support, and show interest in your child's sport (even if you secretly have little interest in it), the closer your bond, and the fonder the memories will be with your child-athlete.

Motivate your children to keep a journal of their thoughts. Ask them to write down what they like about themselves, what they wish to improve on, and tell them to review their progress every month and give themselves a "grade." If they want to improve in an area in which you have talent, take the time to help your child. There is nothing more disheartening than knowing you fall short in an area and do not have the skills or tools to improve even though the desire to do so is present. As a parent be aware of your children's feelings of accomplishment, but also understand their lack of competency concerns.

My older son, who became an advanced math student in junior high, felt insecure about his math skills during his childhood. My younger son bemoans the fact that he is not a bigger-boned kid because he wanted to continue in the football program. Each has now found their personal way. My older son practiced and began to excel in a masterful way in math and was accepted into a competitive engineering program, although he has now decided to study philosophy. My younger son has taken up volleyball. He is excellent and greatly enjoys the sport and the friendships with his teammates.

I tell my children, "We are born in America with equal rights, at least we should be, but not with equal abilities in every area, and that is fine; we each find our own path." My mom would say, "You need to go and find your spot in *the sunshine." Through education and hard work, many things are possible.*

I do tell my children that education is their door to many life choices, but they cannot be absolutely "anything" they want to be because I think it is an exaggerated and unrealistic mantra. Some folks would disagree with my tactics; I started to be more realistic when they became more critical thinkers. I would love to sing opera, but I cannot carry a tune, I might learn to improve, but I will not get to perform with the Metropolitan Opera! I am a great believer that some people are born with certain extraordinary musical, artistic, or mathematical gifts, but we all have our own unique ways of excelling and being our best in this world. We need to discover our inimitable talent, passion, and purpose. As parents, we need to support our children's strengths and promote their development to the fullest.

Always encourage your children: letters or cards filled with words of praise, or a special dinner or outing to an event they enjoy are all options of reward for a great report card. However, don't give false praise. I believe strongly in merit; acknowledge the effort. You can commend your kids for hard work even if the outcome is not as brilliant as they or you might have hoped for. However, if the effort is not what it should be and you offer congratulations, then you merely encourage mediocre performance or laziness.

Also, this past era of parents feeling that any criticism negatively affected their child's fragile self-esteem is ludicrous. I am one parent who feels it created a false image of the world. In the outside world, people are rewarded for effort and good work; and honest competition is everywhere. We need to raise children who know that study, research, tenacity, earnestness, and law-abiding behavior is what will garner praise and rewards. As for those who have succeeded through ill-gotten means, I believe that for many of them, downfall awaits. For those who continue on, I wonder how their other primary relationships function. I believe that a person who "embezzles" in their professional life does so in their private life as well, and the reciprocal often holds true.

- *Teach your children that success is not just how much money they earn but how happy they feel at their core and how content they are with their family, friends, and life choices.*

- *Try to always keep your promises, and don't make any you don't intend to keep. This practice will reflect in their present and future behavior toward you and others. If you do change plans, you must explain clearly and carefully why; and you must arrange to reschedule, or do something comparable.*

- *Make family albums together, speak about your ancestors, give children a sense of continuity, even in less intact families (of which there certainly are many these days). There is a story to be told, understood, and treasured.*

- *Draw with your child; or send him or her to an art class, or go together. My son loved to bring home his creations. It solved the "what to get Mom for her birthday and Mother's Day" dilemma.*

- *Bake and cook as a team, share meals, do laundry together, and give each child a chore. Young men may complain initially if you start this too late in their education process, but they will benefit from learning the fundamentals of knowing how to feed themselves and care for their own home. If they do marry, you will have a happier daughter-in-law!*

- *Create a picnic—whether it is outdoors or on a blanket indoors with potted flowers arranged around the floor. You can feature a culinary creation by each child.*

- *From an early age, post a "Responsibility Board." Chores can be both unrewarded and rewarded. Some types of work should be part of the family unit; perhaps you can create others where the child volunteers and earns money; or maybe a trip to a movie, or extra television or computer time. Chores that do not get done should warrant demerits; I believe that poor behavior should elicit consequences, such as a loss of privileges.*

- *If you are a religious family, worshipping together is a wonderful time to discuss values or just share time. Perhaps go on a "pilgrimage" to a holy place.*

- *The economy has been difficult for many, devastating for others. Find a community center, or offer to volunteer in exchange for your children's participation in an art or athletic program.*

- *Model altruistic behavior early; your children can donate a few of their birthday gifts every year to a children's charity or hospital. You can bring your kids to visit and participate at a shelter. One friend brought her daughters to a shelter every Saturday where they packed brown bags with food for the homeless and poor families; her girls enjoyed the feeling of satisfaction so much they continued this practice until they went off to college. Teach your children to save some of whatever they earn or receive as an allowance, and share a part with those less fortunate. At the end of the year, send it to a worthwhile organization or donate the funds in person. The habit of learning to save will serve them well later in life, and the charity will give your child a sense of empowerment, knowing that each of us can have an impact on the world as a result of our deeds and actions. My family foundation has organized an event for almost thirty years for Meals on Wheels that feeds the homebound hungry. My boys have attended every event, and my older son has delivered meals. Your family can "adopt" a cause!*

- *Thanksgiving is a great day to deliver meals to the needy, so why not work in a shelter that day with your children and celebrate on your own a bit later, or the following day!*

- *If you try to perform at least one random act of kindness every day, your children will follow suit. They must understand that their acts do not have to be directed to someone they know. Doing good feels good, they will be happier people in general, and you will be as well!*

- *If you have the means to help a family, either financially or with your time, do so. You will find yourself being enlightened and uplifted. You can also "share" the family you wish to aid with a couple of other families, which will spread the cost and the time commitments. If you can include your children in the process, it will enrich their lives enormously.*

I have three foster children in India whom I sponsor with funds; however, I know from the orphanage director that they look forward to the letters and photos I send with great anticipation; these words of encouragement are food for the soul for these children. My younger son has written a letter to the boy (the other two are girls). Two have handicaps, all three are very poor, yet they all speak about how important their education is to them.

Becoming a penpal or fostering a child in the U.S. or another country is a wonderful way for your child to learn about other cultures. Through communication and the process of helping another human being, your children will start to realize that although nourishment, a home, an education, and a loving adult to care for them is what every child deserves, many do not have these very basic elements to ensure a healthy, secure, or promising future. The words spoken by these children may prove more powerful than anything I might say about poverty to my sons, and how we must live with gratitude for all the blessings we have.

"Don't measure yourself
by what you have accomplished,
but by what you should have
accomplished with your ability."

—JOHN WOODEN, MEMBER
OF THE BASKETBALL HALL OF FAME
AS BOTH A PLAYER AND COACH

"A recipe for success: perspiration
and heart; blended with education,
talent, experience, a pinch of opportunity,
and a large dollop of respect for
others rights and feelings."

—BARBARA LAZAROFF

For You, I Wish

A Walk on the Beach

I walked the sandy shores of the Atlantic today, in awe that no matter the state, country, or continent, a walk next to salty waters brings about a sense of calm and serenity. I thought of you and wondered if I am doing my job correctly. Your world, moving at a pace I cannot fathom, is filled with electronics and peer pressure. Can I compete? Can I inspire you? When you look to the horizon, do you contemplate the world beyond? Do you marvel at the sun's reflection glistening across the water? Do you think about the endless life swimming below?

Stop, child, let me open your mind. Scoop up a handful of sand and let it run through your fingers, mesmerizing you by its feel. Become amazed by the uniqueness of a seashell washed to shore. Let me compete with your world. Watch a flock of birds soar above and question their line formation. Ponder the tide coming and going and its relationship to the moon and then I will know I am doing my job right. I question, can I compete with the wonders of your world with the wonders of mine? Explore these marvels and never forget that when a stranger shares your walk, smile and say "Hello." I recognize that my job with you is plentiful, but if I can show you some of this, I know we are off to a good start. For you, I wish a walk on the beach.

"The hardest part about showing children the wonders of the world is first spotting them ourselves."

—TRICIA LaVOICE

❊ Reflection ❊

The hardest part about showing children the wonders of the world is first spotting them ourselves. It is easy to get caught up in the pressures of life, the fast pace, and to lose focus in the exhaustion of it all. Nature greatly inspired my father, so I was fortunate to be raised finding wonder in my world as a child. This was one of the greatest gifts my father offered me. We would go on walks together quite often, and he would always point out what amazed him—such as a shadow cast by a tree or the beautiful craftsmanship of a spider web. He would ask me where I thought the sun was going as it waved goodnight to me and would talk about the lightning bugs filling the summer night's sky. He gave me a sense of wonder about my world that could never be taken away.

It is easy to overlook so many of Mother Nature's miracles, but when we take a moment to think about them, they are endless. I try to point them out to my children, just as my father did for me. To plant a seed in the garden is a wonderful task to share, but to first place the seed in a child's hand and express the fascination that this little seed will grow under the earth while we sleep, sprout in the spring, and bring us food or beauty makes the whole task that much more valuable for them.

I do not know what life will bring to my children, whether they will find love; and have good fortune and good health. I can prepare them for their futures to the best of my ability and pray for the best, but I cannot control it. By opening their eyes to the miracles of life, teaching them to not take anything for granted, I am assured that they will always have a moon in their sky to watch wane and wax, and bees in their gardens to pollinate the flowers. Rich or poor, alone or with families of their own, the wonder of life will always be waiting for them outside their doors if they know how to see it. I make mistakes in my parenting every day and am constantly learning about being a mom, but knowing that I am giving my children the gift of wonderment offers me comfort that they are going to be just fine.

"Every corner of our world has
a surprise to offer; it shares those gifts
with all of us. We just need to look, and
take the time to see, to really appreciate
what is before us: to listen and truly hear;
to feel, and enjoy so many sensations; to
breathe deeply and inhale the aroma of
life. Discover your walk on the beach, your
climb to a mountaintop, your moment in
the sun, and bask. Even in the smallest
of spaces there is the mystery of nature
and the power of the spirit that shares it."

—BARBARA LAZAROFF

Words and Actions from Barbara

May you remember your journeys and lessons of life always, so that one day you can realize how many steps you have taken, how high you have climbed, and how many lives you have touched. Along the way, remember as parents that one of your missions is to inspire your children's journeys and teach them to witness and appreciate the miracles of life. These lessons will help them remember that we must protect the natural magnificence of our world.

- *When on the East Coast, get up early and take your child to watch the sunrise. It's especially wonderful if you can get to a beach and watch it rise over the ocean.*

- *Watch the sunset. Look for the final glow as the sun disappears and make a wish. If on the West Coast, this is a beautiful experience to watch over the Pacific Ocean.*

- *Research "full moons" and note how the moon wanes and waxes all month long.*

- *Lie on your backs together, looking up at the sky. Discover interesting shapes in the clouds.*

- *One evening look up at the sky and find patterns in the stars. Teach your child about the various constellations. Wish.*

- *Sit and watch an army of ants at work.*

- *Watch the bees fly from one flower to the next. Talk about pollination.*

- *Just admire the fascinating patterns of a spider web.*

- *Plant sunflower seeds together. When they grow, see how the sunflower faces turn throughout the day to follow the sun.*

- *There are many breathtaking shows on television about the wonders of nature. Watch them with your children and point out what captivates you. Ask them what particularly moves them, and if they would like to learn more about that subject.*

- *Skip rocks down by a river or lake.*

- *Visit the wonders of an aquarium, a planetarium, a zoo, or a natural-habitat museum. Read about the environments you are to visit with your children (and their friends, perhaps). Study a bit about some of the animals or plants prior to the trip, as this will inspire your children to ask questions. Perhaps find a guide at these locations; they will be passionate and knowledgeable about their areas of expertise. If the location is too large to cover in one day, find out which areas are most appropriate to visit first for your child's age.*

- *Take a walk around the neighborhood and attempt to identify neighbors' plants and flowers. You could take a camera, photograph the flora, and look them up on the internet. You can make signs for your garden areas; plant nurseries sell small identifiers to post on which you can write waterproof ink. Have your children help make a personal botanical garden. Plant a vegetable and herb garden; this provides a time of delight; particularly as their crops come in!*

- *Go snorkeling, or if you can afford it and are adventurous, learn to scuba dive together. Explore caves, take nature hikes, collect specimens of shells and rocks, or start a collection. Collect and identify flora; make a book of pressed flowers and plants. Watch out for the poison ivy!*

- *Create a more beautiful world! Organize a group of parents and children to adopt and clean up a park, or a portion of the beach, or perhaps tidy the neighborhood you live in. Plant some flowers on your street. This will give your children a sense of pride as well.*

- *Help out in an animal shelter or a veterinarian's office; volunteer with your child at an "adopt a pet" day. Many children find enormous joy in interacting with animals. These will be memorable days providing much-needed attention and care to these dear creatures. Animals provide unconditional love, and are glorious teachers.*

"Study nature, love nature,
stay close to nature.
It will never fail you."

—FRANK LLOYD WRIGHT, ARCHITECT

"My life is like a stroll on the beach . . .
as near to the edge as I can go."

—THOREAU, POET AND AUTHOR

"To myself I am only a child playing
on the beach, while vast oceans of truth
lie undiscovered before me."

—ISAAC NEWTON, SCIENTIST

For You, I Wish

The Sky

Beautiful boy hiding behind your coat of armor, the world has betrayed you and society robs your gender the right to grieve. Only the salt from your tears can melt your shield, but protect yourself now as you must. It cannot keep me from seeing your watering eyes, feeling your hurting heart. You feel vulnerable and exposed, naked in a cold world with many roads to travel, holding only a broken compass. Remember, when learning to walk, you fell again and again and I was there to pick you up, but then you fell again and you alone pulled yourself to safety. You cried from your bed and I came to soothe you; you cried again and you alone soothed yourself back to slumber.

Beneath your metal coat, you possess the strength to see yourself through. What you don't know, my beautiful boy, is that while you were picking yourself up, I was moving furniture from your way, and as you soothed yourself back to sleep, I was lying on the floor at the foot of your bed. Oceans will separate us, mountains will divide us, but I am always with you. When you wake up in the morning, look to the sun and let it warm your face, knowing I am looking to the same sun. In the early evening, look to the stars and wish, knowing I am wishing on the same stars. And most of all, my beautiful boy, look to the sky and know my love for you. There is no beginning, no end, no start, no finish; my love is everywhere—behind you, in front of you, to the sides of you. I wish you the sky of my love, grand and infinite, always and forever.

"There is no beginning, no end, no start, no finish; my love is everywhere."

—TRICIA LaVOICE

❋ Reflection ❋

I recently read a statistic that one in four or five women, I can't re-member exactly, would rather be a man than a woman. Thinking about this option, I concluded for myself that no matter how easy it makes camping or getting ready to go out at night, no matter what the benefits in the workplace are, I could not imagine living a life where my emotions could not run free.

This winter, my family and I watched a lot of the Olympics together, and I must have gotten teary ten times over the two-week period. I cried watching the parents swell up over their children's victories, I cried with the athlete who won and lost, and as most observers, I cried watching the ice skater compete only two days after her mother passed away. I also shed many tears watching the horrific piece on the bobsledder who had a fatal accident during practice the day before the events began. My children really did not even pay attention to me and my tears. I love to be free to not only watch the athletes, but to be emotionally engaged, to experience a taste of the passion they must all be feeling. I am not sure how it would have gone over if it were one of my sons or my husband who showed this much emotion during the games. I suspect we all may have been alarmed. Does this mean males feel any less? Have we condi-tioned them to be less sensitive?

Recently, we had a couple visiting us who had twin five-year-olds, a boy and a girl. The couple started parenting late in life, and although they get physically exhausted easily, they have the advantage of parent-ing with more life experiences than the rest of us. At one time during their visit, the little boy fell and hurt himself, but not too badly. He ran to his father, who picked him up and held him, and he whispered to him, "Go ahead and cry, let it out." I loved seeing the sensitivity shared between father and son, when I had expected to hear him say, "You're okay," which I would have thought was the appropriate response before I heard the more sensitive one given.

It is easy to get a five-year-old who has been raised to express his emotions to communicate his feelings, but by the time our boys are young men, a shield goes up for many, making it hard to reach them.

These bottled-up feelings usually have a tendency to manifest themselves in ugly ways, which is no good for anyone. Although our sons will act as if they do not want to talk to us, which is probably true, it is very important that we express our love to them. They must understand that we are there standing still and available at any given moment if they need us. When they pretend their hearts are not hurting, we must speak of a hurting heart and validate the emotion that we know they are suppressing. They will tell us to go away and shut the doors, but they will hear us. When we are fortunate enough to get them to open up to us, we must be very careful with the words we choose, for the shield is quick to go back up.

Boys are so wonderful and loving, and when raised with sensitivity, grow to be fabulous husbands and fathers themselves. Love them and talk to them, for shields of armor may provide refuge, but they are not soundproof.

Words and Actions from Barbara

Dr. Seuss proclaimed, "A person's a person, no matter how small." Therefore, I believe that a betrayal, a disappointment, a family relocation, a broken heart, the death of a beloved pet, or the profound loss of a loved one can feel as painful to a small person, or a young adult, as to an adult. We often believe that our children will heal because they have youth and the passage of time on their side. Often that is very true, and in many cases the slights and failures they experience are not life altering and will often be forgotten in the broader landscape of their lives. However, there are certain rainstorms that may blacken their psyches, "their skies," for years to come.

Tricia wrote this Wish for one of my sons at a particularly difficult juncture in his life. His heart had been broken and he had come to realize that a person he had trusted with his innermost feelings was disloyal. It was a moment I could relate to, but of course this was *his* pain, his moment, his loss. My job as a mother was to try to support him as best I could, and this varied depending on the day of the week, the time of day, and his point in the healing process. Basically, I was on call. Occasionally it was exhausting; however, his trust in my love for him became an opportunity to bond.

- *Try to speak with your children every day about what is going on in their lives. Ask about school and other interests. They likely will not offer as much information as they get older, but at least they know you care. When they are at the noncommunicative stage in their development, be patient, be understanding, and try to restrain yourself from being overbearing with your concern. Let them know you are always open to hearing them. Your teenage children may be critical, and feel you are as well. They will only truly know what it feels like to be a concerned parent when they have their own children. I have therefore stopped trying to explain myself!*

- *Do not be intimidated about discussing drugs, alcohol, sex, and other issues that may be uncomfortable not only for your child, but for you as well. Start communicating when they are young so that they are comfortable discussing these topics. I started talking to my boys early in their development, delicately at first and with greater detail as they got older.*

- *Learn to communicate on their terms. One of my sons does not answer his cell phone or respond to his e-mail too often; when he lost his computer it then made e-mails impossible! He did text, however, so I took up his form of communication and taught my mom how to text as well so that she could "talk" to him at college.*

- *Send care packages of their favorite cookies, a hand-knit cap or scarf, amusing cards, a little fun money, a recent family photo from home of their pet or sibling.*

- *If you are deeply concerned about your children's well-being, call their closest friends to check up and express your concerns. They may offer some helpful suggestions.*

- *If your children are away or living on their own, let them know they have a ticket and a place at home anytime they need the comfort and safety of their family.*

- *When our children are small, we can play games such as "What was the best moment of your day and what was your worst?" It is amazing what they will share and what you will learn about their concerns, fears, and hopes. Remember, keeping communication flowing requires consistent exchanges of ideas with an open mind; this needs to start very early.*

- *Ask your children to draw a picture of the best day of the week, and describe it; you do this as well. This is particularly effective with younger children.*

- *Relate some stories from your own childhood about embarrassing moments, disappointments, things that frightened you, moments of failure, and times of achievement. My mom told me some of the funniest stories, and I have since asked her to tell my children. One truly memorable anecdote in particular was about a strict chorus teacher who was horrid to her and the other children. The teacher was only concerned about making a good impression on the parents. When the day of the big auditorium performance arrived, she would not let one of the boys go to the bathroom. As the chorus began to sing, he could not restrain himself any longer, and he started to relieve himself while thirty other children followed onstage! This story always made me feel better no matter what embarrassing moment I experienced as a child!*

- *It is extremely important for you to get professional advice for your child if you suspect a serious emotional or physical problem. If you are confused about whether or not some issue is merely an age-appropriate behavior, or a signpost of a possible underlying illness, ask friends, family members, and consult with counselors with respect to what they see and feel about your child's behavioral patterns or responses in certain situations. However, as the mother, you are usually the best judge of your child's needs. There are those instances where parents are in denial: a father who would not believe his son was autistic, a mother I know who could not admit to herself that her preteen son was smoking, and another whose son was using her prescription drugs. The sooner you deal with a problem, the sooner you can make progress toward raising a healthy, productive child.*

- *Help your child develop a strong E.Q. (emotional quotient or emotional I.Q.). We spend an enormous amount of time and finances on the intellectual development of our children, but studies now reveal that a person's E.Q. may be just as important, if not more vital, to the overall success of individuals developing healthy personal and professional relationships. There are many books and online informational studies and videos about the importance of E.Q.; as well as seminars and tutorials on how to train our children, and ourselves, in expanding these skills. Self-awareness, self-management, social awareness, and relationship management all require learning both verbal and nonverbal cues, conflict resolution, stress reduction, controlling impulsive feelings and behaviors—all necessary tools and skills for survival in order to live long and well.*

- *Support your children; and be a cheerleader and a nurturer, but if you truly want the best for them, you will not minimize the responsibility of disciplining them. You may be looking at the same sky, but remember to remind them that if they want to fly straight and strong and arrive at their destinations, they must open their hearts, keep their minds and bodies healthy, cast off their protective masks, and live life bravely and fully. They know you will always be on their team; however, it is ultimately their own strengths, independence, and choices that will be the defining factors with respect to where they land.*

"Each friend represents a world
in us, a world possibly not born until
they arrive, and it is only by this
meeting that a new world is born."

—ANAÏS NIN, AUTHOR

For You, I Wish

Your Bloom

My child, you are a bud in bloom but growing so fast, I yearn to slow the rain and sun that encourages you. Soon you will be a beautiful flower off dazzling the world far from my view. Never forget that you are my rose; if you sit on the table or rest in the garden, if basking in the moonlight or lazing in the sunshine, you are my rose. Move forward with your elegance, but remain alert; life is not always a bed of roses. There will be times when the wind and rain knock your petals to the ground. Stay strong; you cannot be defeated if you are creating potpourri. Your sister roses will come in shapes and colors special for them; respect their differences and rejoice in the array of splendor you create together. Let your beauty grace the eye, let your fragrance perfume the air, but take care not to wound with your thorns. Life may not always be a bed of roses, but life is beautiful; and you, my child, are always my rose.

For you, I wish your bloom.

"It has been said: 'Use what talents you possess: the woods would be very silent if no birds sang there except those that sang best.'"

—Henry Van Dyke, author

❋ ❋ ❋

"I tell all my goddaughters they are unique and exceptional, each in their own singular way. They constantly delight and surprise me with their assorted abilities. They may not be the most graceful ballerinas, or the sweetest singers, or the most eloquent writers, or the most powerful athletes, but I enthusiastically support their dreams. Each has a personal story still budding, and they should develop and express it with all their heart, mind, and might, to full bloom. They are the future; and together, their ideas, voices, and actions will change the world."

—Barbara Lazaroff

❋ Reflection ❋

The relationship shared between mother and daughter will be the most influential relationship of a daughter's life. Letting a daughter know she is loved by her mother unconditionally is essential for her to be able to love herself and love others, while having the self-esteem she will need to thrive in today's world. As she becomes a wife, mother, and friend to others, the love she received and continues to receive from her own mother will give her the strength, courage, and wisdom she needs to succeed in these relationships. And yet, there are many other lessons that must be taught; and although she will listen to what her mother <u>says</u>, mostly she will copy what her mother <u>does</u>. Telling her that gossip is not nice will have little effect on her if she hears her mother gossiping. Verbally emphasizing the importance of education to her is wonderful, but seeing her mother read a book is more effective. She needs to see her mother's compassion, feel her mother's confidence, and witness her mother's self-respect so that she, in turn, will have it for herself.

I love, love, love raising a daughter, although I admit that it scares me. I want to protect her from the world, yet I know I cannot. I would never sleep another wink if I allowed myself to think about all the possible dangers to a young girl, so I try to simply trust that she <u>is</u> okay and <u>will be</u> okay. Some may consider me neurotic, but I just consider myself a mother.

Being creative and having fun while teaching our daughters life lessons can be good for everyone. One of my favorite books is <u>The Red Tent</u> by Anita Diamant, which tells the story of women in biblical times. What fascinates me most about the women in this book is the glorious celebration they hold for young girls when they begin to menstruate, marking their ability to give birth. After proper ritual, the girls are honored into the tent with the other women, where they gather once a month and to give birth.

I thought of all the events and birthdays I celebrated with my daughter and questioned why this amazing milestone should slip through the cracks without tribute. I also hoped that by celebrating her first menstrual cycle, it would not only stress the gift of childbearing, but also the responsibility that went along with this power.

My friends were on alert, and we waited for Olivia's period to come. When it finally did, she was a sport and only slightly resisted the attention, allowing my wonderful friend Carlene to host a "Red Tent" party. All my girlfriends joined in the fun and dressed up in flowing gauze dresses, bringing presents to share in this welcoming of Olivia into womanhood. I rented two beautiful Moroccan tents, which we set up in Carlene's yard overlooking the Los Angeles skyline. We kept Olivia and her five friends in the smaller tent while about twenty-five of us women prepared the party in the larger tent. As the sun set, we gathered outside the girls' tent and took turns sharing words of wisdom with them. Then we all returned to the larger tent and partied the night away with good food and song.

I am not sure if the celebration influenced Olivia's perception, but I do know we had a ton of fun and it was important to me to recognize this significant occasion in her life. Raising a daughter comes with many challenges—but how amazing it is to watch a flower in bloom!

"To the buds, when you bloom, you will be the women who will educate the next generation of girls and boys. You will make global policy; grow food; find cures; create art, music and dance; and hopefully end wars. Learn, grow, blossom, and give back. Leave a forest of love and knowledge behind you."

—BARBARA LAZAROFF

Words and Actions from Barbara

I always tell my girlfriends and their daughters to prepare for their lives (I learned that as a Brownie). Instruct your daughters to study, listen well, observe carefully, travel, and seek out mentors. So often in the past, and even presently, young women are defined in terms of their external beauty. There is nothing as enduring as internal loveliness and strength gathered from education, experience, and enlightenment. Certainly, we want our young women to better themselves professionally through networking organizations, or by getting a degree or advanced degree; however, there is also much personal benefit to be achieved through helping others through charity. One of my favorite proverbs is: "A bit of fragrance always clings to the hand that gives you roses."

If women hope to produce a world of strong, proficient sisterhood, education is the first step to a better life; and team work is the other. I have often said, "We are a sisterhood. One woman's success is every woman's success, and we are all strengthened when we extend our hands and help another young woman along the path."

- *It is essential to have credit in your own name. Tell your friends to do the same, even if they are married.*

- *Be prepared as best you can, emotionally and educationally, to be able to provide for yourself and your children in the future. If you develop well-honed intellectual and personal skills and tools, you can survive the loss of a job or a divorce and will be flexible and resilient enough to refocus and pursue a new life path.*

- *Always remember, too, that you are blessed in life. We all go through tough times; remarkably, some of the struggles in our lives turn into opportunities. Be grateful for the gifts you do have; keeping a positive attitude attracts greater possibilities.*

- *You must exert energy and work moment by moment to fashion your own destiny. Be confident in your abilities, but continue to work diligently on overcoming your weaknesses.*

For You, I Wish

Your Way

I anger you; you flail your arms and gulp water as you struggle to stay afloat. You see me standing on the ocean's edge, holding the life preserver that has saved you so many times before. I watch the current pull you farther from safety. You reach out your arms to me, but I remain still. You must move now. I can no longer hold you up, so hold my words close. Remain alert; the waters can change at any time. Swim with the current as much as possible and let its energy move you. When it gets choppy, swim harder; when you are too tired to swim another stroke, swim your hardest. When you hit a riptide, stay calm. Watch out for sharks and barracudas. Your heart pounds and you tread water, not moving from your place. But rest assured the ocean is grand and full of beauty. It can take you around the world and back. The salt of its waters will heal your wounds, and the fish from its core will nourish your body. If you trust and relax, you will float much of your journey, you will see an array of beauty in color and form. Remember to swim like the dolphins jumping through the air, glide like a sea turtle, dream like a mermaid.

Over the years, spend time in a school of fish; swim solo like a beluga whale. You see me standing on the water's edge holding a life preserver and you are confused as to why I do not toss it your way. Know that my arms tremble in resistance. You are frightened and so am I. I yearn to swallow the seven seas so you can walk to safety; I yearn to battle every creature known to the ocean's water. I must let you go now and wish you on your way, but of all my words, hold these words closest: I stand apart from you now, watching from the ocean's edge, but I am prepared, and if you lose your way, I will swim around the globe in hunt for you. This I promise. For you, I wish your way.

"One day it became clear that
they were their own persons.
These were their lives, their journeys."

—TRICIA LaVOICE

❋ Reflection ❋

I am not sure how many of us really know what parenting is all about when we first decide to start a family. I, for one, did not. I remember wanting sweet little babies that I could hold and play with and dress in cute clothes. They were MY babies, MY children, and then one day it became clear that they were their own persons, these were their lives, their journeys. The thought was actually overwhelming for me. It is one thing to make mistakes with MY children, but making mistakes with someone else's life is a completely different story. One day you're concerned with getting them into a good preschool and having them use good manners so that everyone sees that YOUR children are well behaved, and then the next, you suddenly realize that they feel emotional pain, they fear, and they experience self-doubt. The responsibility is huge: making sure they grow up liking themselves—capable of handling hardships while having limited anxieties. And then, there is love and our never-ending influence on how they will perceive it, accept it, and bestow it.

Preparing our children to become adults takes hard work, trust, and courage. Chances are, they will encounter heartbreaks, difficult bosses, and callous co-workers throughout their lives, and we will not be there to fight their battles and protect them. It is our responsibility to love them, prepare them, and let them live their own lives. Our greatest challenge is in discovering how to do just that.

By letting them make mistakes and experience emotional pain, our children learn the lessons in life that give them the self-confidence, self-assurance, and self-esteem we want them to have as adults. I like to look at universal conditions as nature's way of telling me when to pay attention. If my child were the only child experiencing hardships and dealing with playground politics, I would worry much more. However, when I see all the children experiencing similar trials and tribulations, I believe it is nature's way of letting them practice before adulthood.

This did not always come so easy to me. I remember the first time Olivia came home from kindergarten crying about another child. I was just about to call the bully's mother when my sister called me and talked me down. Luckily for me, my sisters and Rich's sisters all have older kids, so I get to benefit from their experiences when I am open to listening.

My sister explained that this was just the beginning of the drama with friends that my daughter would bring home over the years, and I should remember that there are always two sides to every story. I certainly could not be getting involved and calling mothers all my life, so it would be much better to guide her in handling her own battles. I learned to get involved only when my intervention is truly needed, and to let my children take responsibility for, and control of, their personal lives.

Preparing our children for adulthood is by no means easy—but it is crucial. I would have had a dozen kids if all I had to do was love them like I did when they were babies. Holding them is easy; letting them go is the difficult part.

"You can be the glorious dandelion on the winds of time that sends out messages of hope, creating change, making your dreams come true, and enlightening those around you."

—BARBARA LAZAROFF

Words and Actions from Barbara

So many people in our culture judge success in terms of the clothes you have on your back, what kind of car you're driving, or where you live. I enjoy beautiful things and I do collect things, but only later in life do you realize that these things don't necessarily bring you happiness. What I want my boys to remember:

- *Never forget your family responsibilities, and honor yourself as well. These are your first priorities.*

- *Working toward success in every aspect of life is a never-ending task. Professional success can be fleeting if you are not on top of your work and the changing technologies and zeitgeist. Remember, if you measure success in terms of financial gain or status alone, to the exclusion of family and friendship, you may be disappointed to find your life less fulfilling than you imagined.*

- *Some people believe if marriage or friendship is work, it isn't worth it. Untrue! All relationships require reviews and adjustments.*

- *We change, life changes, and to stay together, you have to be committed to communication, compromise; and sustaining the family unit, your friendships, and your professional relationships. However, if you are not cherished, respected or appreciated, you must know when to move on.*

- *Surround yourself with doers who have purpose and heart; learn from them, participate, add value, and they will guide you. Shrug off the users, the manipulators, and the naysayers.*

- *Stand up straight—your emotional and physical "posture" affects everything. Attitude has more to do with your day than the actual events of the day. How you respond to your environment changes it—change it for the better, no matter what comes your way.*

- *Think and act responsibly; what you say and do affects so many; and these individuals, in turn, affect others. Excess in alcohol or food, lack of sleep, and other personal abuses does not bode well for your prime performance, and negatively affects others.*

For You, I Wish

Your Place Among Women

I was born a child to the clan, a pack animal, a social creature. Always at my mother's side until the day she whispered, "Go, child, sit with your sisters by the fire. Find your place among women." There I formed my thoughts, my values, my way. I found safety, purpose, love. As we grew tall, we laughed together, ventured beyond our camps, shared visions and dreams. As we grew taller, we stood at each other's sides as we wed and birthed. The children scurried off to play as the men went off to hunt. My sisters shadowed my children, fed my husband as I theirs. Kindred spirits, we worked together to nurture our people.

Then one morning, I awoke to find myself missing. My first family and I separated from our kin. We walked the woods alone. Soon my children scurried off to play and my mate to hunt. Lost without my sisters, I cried my eyes blue. Defined by their words, dependent on their guidance, I stumbled in their absence. Was I too reliant? Maybe. Left with no choice, I picked myself up alone. I gained a self-respect, a wisdom that only could be found in my loneliness. Yet, for every one step I took in self-pride, I took two in missing them; for every one step I took in newfound insight, I took two in wishing time backward. Isolation became part of my journey with much to offer, yet I did not need it to remind me that I was born a child of the clan, a pack animal, a social creature.

I now whisper to daughters of all clans, "Go, child, sit with your sisters by the fire. Find your place among women. Trust her and earn her trust; you will see clearer and find your feet planted to the ground for this: love her and let her love you; you will be a better mother and wife for this; care for her and she will, in return, care for you. When in her presence, put away all jealousies, competitions, and betrayals. You may choose to walk alone, but see through my eyes, when you walk with your sisters, the journey is simpler and so much sweeter." For you, I wish you your place among women.

"It is never too soon or too late
to find your place among women."

—Tricia LaVoice

❁ Reflection ❁

It wasn't long after we moved to Connecticut that I was standing in line at a coffee shop, waiting my turn, and overheard a conversation between two young girls. They looked like they were about thirteen or fourteen years old, and from the look of their outfits, had just come from riding lessons. There was no effort to eavesdrop on my part, for they spoke loudly and clearly, as if proud of what they were saying. Their conversation gained momentum and vengeance as they gossiped away about another girl at the barn. They criticized her riding abilities, her outfits, and even her horse. I was glad when I saw the mother turn to them, hoping she would put an end to the noise pollution, but I was shocked when she joined in and began gossiping herself. There was no talk of tolerance, forgiveness, compassion, or the evils of judgment.

Growing up with girlfriends and having girlfriends as an adult woman is a priceless gift. But a friendship is a relationship and, like all relationships, they take time and effort. You have to have each other's backs. You must have love, loyalty, respect, trust, and acceptance. You must be able to forgive and work through the fights, no matter how petty or serious, if you hope to maintain true, deep friendships. Teaching our daughters the importance of being a good friend and having good friends will offer them a lifetime of support and love.

But women will play other roles in our daughters' lives, and it is important that our daughters know how to get along with them. They may have sisters-in-law, mothers-in-law; they will most likely have female co-workers and maybe a female boss. Female mentors are huge. I started collecting them when I was young, with my big sister Liz being my first, and now have an array of women mentors who have taught me more about life than all my college courses combined.

Learning how to get along with other women comes very easily for some and is more challenging for others. However, all women benefit from having female friends—those you want to sit up with all night long and talk to, friends to hold your secrets, to tell you not to worry, and friends to cry to when life gets too hard. Our girlfriends are our rocks when we are unsteady, our light when things are dark. Having *girlfriends is a treasure, and we must stress to our daughters the importance of having these friendships throughout their lives. The best way to ensure this is to begin by teaching our daughters how to be good girlfriends themselves. The best way to teach them this concept is letting them watch us being our genuine selves.*

"Go, child, sit with your sisters by the fire. Find your place among women."

—TRICIA LaVOICE

Words and Actions from Barbara

Ambition rocks, treachery does not! Other women are your sisters. Treat them with respect—with the same respect you would like to receive. Don't underestimate a less experienced sister; you may be working for her one day! Ways to join the sisterhood:

- *Explore a professional association or social networking group pertaining to your career and interests such as the National Association of Women Business Owners. Join up and participate!*

- *Connect with organizations that are already a part of your life. For example, if you have children, try joining the PTA, or become a leader for a Girl Scout troop.*

- *Meet great women while helping others. Volunteer at a local hospital, participate in walk-a-thons and charity tournaments, and read to the young or elderly. Scouting for volunteering opportunities in your area affords you the ability to meet other like-minded women. Involve your daughter in some of these activities; you can spend meaningful time together, and it will positively affect her future behavior toward others in need.*

- *Instructing a young girl how to swim, knit, use a computer, bake, ride a bike, open a savings account, or properly organize a research paper is an immense gift of self-confidence that will affect the rest of her life.*

- *On the fun side of meeting sisters, join a book club or dare to start one.*

- *If you are the athletic type: join a gym, swim club, play in a tennis or golf tournament, take up yoga, or organize a group hiking retreat.*

- *Start a professional organization; I founded a group with seven other women nearly seventeen years ago, and there are thousands of members now supporting a terrific networking system, and continuing education and scholarship programs. (Some of these professional organizations are listed at the end of my biography.)*

- *Serve on a nonprofit board or a committee; or if you are asked, feel equipped and can afford the time, serve on a corporate board. You will meet other accomplished women with similar or differing interests; network for business as well as friendship.*

Learn how to recognize the manipulator, or the home or job wrecker. Do not get intimate with women who step on others to "get ahead"; if they can do it to another woman in business, or have relations with a married man, lie to their colleagues, take credit for other people's work, or are abusive to assistants and people in positions of service, beware! If they have no conscience about being deceitful with others, they may betray you next. Befriend women of integrity; don't be impressed by the glamour or status of a woman if there is no underlying substance.

"Be a genuine sister, mother, friend: find your place among women. It is indeed a noble place to be."

— BARBARA LAZAROFF

"There is a special place in hell for women who do not help other women."

—Madeleine K. Albright,
Former U.S. Ambassador to the United Nations,
and former Secretary of State

For You, I Wish

A Season of Love

If I could write you spring, I would compose a rainbow and stretch it near and far for you to climb and witness the Seven Wonders of the World. If I could write you summer, I would compose a rushing river and float you to the sea where you could sing with the mermaids and ride the backs of seahorses. If I could write you autumn, I would compose you into an artist so your brush could glide across a colorful landscape creating a new earth. If I could write you winter, I would compose you a snowflake to float you high above the clouds so you could soar throughout the stars. But I do not know how to write you spring and summer or winter and fall. I cannot compose rainbows and rivers or snowflakes and artists. All I know is how to write you love, to compose for you the words of my heart, the whispers of my dreams, to hold your hand in mine, and love you. For you, I wish a season of love.

"I must trust the world to be kind
to my children, and when it is not,
I will be there waiting with open arms."

—Tricia LaVoice

❋ Reflection ❋

If only we held magic in our hands to grant their dreams and protect our children from harm. But life does not work that way. I remember being so prepared for the birth of our first child, Olivia. I read all the right books, attended the seminars, and had plenty of experience baby-sitting growing up. I was playing with dolls from the moment I could hold one, and now I was getting a real one. I could not stand waiting another minute to kiss her, smell her, and hold her close. I was more prepared to become a mother than anything I had ever done in my life until the reality check hit me like a ton of bricks. I think it was around day five. We were home from the hospital and my mother had returned to her house, leaving Rich and me in charge. I believe it was Olivia's runny nose that had us calling the ER at three in the morning. We were unaware of the vulnerability that came with parenting. There was no way to plan for it. Ten months earlier she was a thought; now she was our entire world. No one can prepare you for the love you will feel, or the fear that goes along with that love.

Now, when I read this Wish, I yearn more than ever to be able to grant my children their dreams, and more important, protect them. About a year ago our youngest son, Bobby, was clearing his throat a lot and shrugging his shoulders. I was e-mailing Leeza trying to describe his symptoms as if they were similar to someone with Tourette's. Double-checking my spelling, I googled "Tourette's" and began reading; onset between the ages of seven and nine, most common in boys, symptoms include clearing of the throat and shrugging of the shoulders. Bobby was eight at the time. Panic rushed through my body as I frantically typed to Leeza, freaking out. She tried to calm me, saying this was just a neurological hiccup and not to worry. But I sat up until four in the morning talking to my sister-in-law, Dorothy, drowning myself in wine. It took weeks to get an appointment with the best neurologist in town. Barbara flew out and went with Rich and me to the appointment. The doctor was very laid back and explained that Bobby most likely had Tourette's and that the next two years would be most telling. Over the last year, Bobby's symptoms waned and waxed. Every time I thought it was a growing pain and behind us, he would start a new tic. As I write this, he is in a phase where he makes little sounds all the time, sweet sounds. I listen to him playing with friends—laughing and having a blast—but all I hear are the sounds in between. I catch myself being angry at silly things and losing my patience with those around me as I accept that Bobby may always have Tourette's. How can I protect him? How can I make his world okay? Then I rethink it, and I see that Bobby is fine. He does not have a childhood illness that threatens his life, nor is he in pain. He is not even bothered by his tics. When I ask him about his tics and if they bother him, he replies, "No, it feels good, but I know it bothers you." He is right. It does bother me, but only because I cannot protect him.

When reading this Wish, I find myself wishing I could paint him a perfect world in which to grow up, where there is no teasing and no syndromes. I want to write him a rainbow and let him swim with the mermaids, but I cannot, just as I could not stop Olivia's nose from running when she was five days old.

I can try to protect my children from the outside world and even from themselves at times, but many things are outside a mother's control. What is in my control is my ability to love my children and hold their hands in mine. Now, I must trust the world to be kind to my children, and when it's not, I will be there waiting with open arms. What more can a mother do?

"I find myself wishing I could paint
him a perfect world in which to
grow up . . . many things are outside a
mother's control. What is in my control
is my ability to love my children
and hold their hands in mine."

—Tricia LaVoice

"A mother is a safe haven, a teacher of good values and principles, a nurturer. A mother is a disciplinarian; a mother does whatever she has to do for her child. A mother gives unconditional and endless love."

—ELLIE LAZAROFF, BARBARA'S MOTHER

Words and Actions from Barbara

"The grass is greener where the grass is watered." Keep reminding those you cherish that they are worthy of love, that you admire them, treasure them, and that you are blessed to have them in your life.

- *Avoid making judgments around your children. The less harshly they judge their world, the less they will see their world judging them.*

- *Read books pertaining to building children's self-esteem.*

- *Teach them skills to become self-reliant, such as cooking, sewing, changing tires on cars, welding, carpentry, plumbing. Let them help you with projects, even when it might slow you down.*

- *The world can be tough, so keep the home a safe place where they trust they can find love and acceptance. Have zero tolerance for sibling name calling and bullying of one another.*

- *Think of creative ways to spend time with your children. Our lives are hectic, but we can turn everyday routines into fun, loving memories simply by "renaming" everyday situations. Call breakfast your morning "tea party." Place their orange juice in a tea cup so that they feel as if they are drinking tea with you before rushing out the door. Get the mail together and try to guess how many letters and bills will be in the box and from whom. While in the car together, listen to the radio and compose new lyrics to an old song.*

"Whatever they grow up to be,
they are still our children, and the one
most important of all things we can
give to them is unconditional love.
Not a love that depends on anything
at all except that they are our children."

—ROSALEEN DICKSON, AUTHOR

For You, I Wish

To Say "I Am Sorry"

I collected all my wishes and packed them safely with my favorite blanket. I had waited anxiously for this August night's sky when stars would shoot across the galaxy showering the dark with light, showering me with wonder. Night fell, but the sky I walked below was absent of dazzle, absent of awe where I could rest my dreams. Unanticipated fog clogged the airways, foiling my hopes of seeing anything tonight but the gray. I awoke to a similar morning sky and spent most of the day inside, avoiding her gloom. Come dusk, I ventured to walk in her gray, willing to at least enjoy the temperature she offered. Within moments of my journey, her clouds parted, her fog lifted, and the sun broke through, streaking my face in warmth. The light graced the surrounding foliage, giving birth to an array of unimaginable greens.

But she did not stop there. She continued decorating her crystal blue landscape in shades of pink and orange, tranquilizing me with her beauty as if she were trying to make up for the gray in which she smothered me in the night before. First, I cast my eyes to the ground in remorse. Then, I lift them to meet yours in truth. I place one hand on my heart to open my soul and reach the other to you in loyalty. My words are few, but I speak in sorrow and ask for your forgiveness. For you, I wish to say "I am sorry."

"Saying 'I am sorry' is beautiful, cleansing, and healthy."

—Tricia LaVoice

❋ Reflection ❋

It may seem unusual to have an "I am sorry" Wish in a book about mothering, but saying "I am sorry" is a big part of being a mother and a daughter. Teaching our children how to say "I am sorry" is very important if we wish them to have long-term, committed relationships in their lives. Today has just begun, and I know that my son Jack is expecting me to watch a movie with him tonight. However, I forgot that I must bring his brother to basketball. He will be unhappy, even with my apology, but hopefully he will feel my sorrow and understand I simply cannot be in two places at one time.

I never gave much thought to teaching "I am sorry" until a few years back when we had a young girl living with us who struggled with it. We worked on this for over a year before she would take responsibility and apologize when it was necessary. I wondered if she grew up having it said to her. Maybe her parents did not make the mistakes I find myself making, but I find a reason to say "I am sorry" every day to at least one of the kids.

There is a lot attached to saying "I am sorry." A sincere apology must be heartfelt and genuine. You cannot worry about protecting your ego when asking for forgiveness. You must allow yourself to be wrong, and not concern yourself with the other person's role in the argument. Saying "I am sorry" is not always easy, but always important for relationships to have trust and the ability grow. I have worked hard to say "I am sorry" without attaching any blame or "buts." I consider myself good at saying "I am sorry," and I think most of my loved ones would agree, except my husband, Rich. He thinks I stink at it. I am still trying to figure that one out. I tease him that maybe it is because I am always right in the marriage—he does not find that funny. I assume my ego gets in the way with him. I know I must continue to work on this, not only for my marriage's sake, but for my children's as well.

Saying "I am sorry" is beautiful, cleansing, and healthy. Helping our children understand the importance of this is a gift they will use throughout their lives. To be vulnerable, self-reflecting, and accepting of your mistakes is part of the self-growth that children will need as *healthy adults. Saying "I am sorry," like finding forgiveness, is a big part of loving someone. We need to say it and we need to hear it. Children need to understand that moms and dads make mistakes. When we do make mistakes and ask forgiveness, they need to grant us that forgiveness and, when deserving, they need to learn to say "I am sorry" as well.*

"I place one hand on my heart to open my soul and reach the other to you in loyalty. My words are few, but I speak in sorrow and ask for your forgiveness."

—TRICIA LaVOICE

"If over time you know that the issue lies with the other person's inability to forgive; forgive yourself and move on."

—BARBARA LAZAROFF

Words and Actions from Barbara

The ability to articulate "I am sorry" is difficult for so many; to apologize out loud directly and genuinely to another person requires courage and humility. It is a phrase we need to teach our children and one they must hear us speak to them and others. When we have engaged in discord with a spouse, a co-worker, a friend, a relative, our child, or our parents, we must separate from our ego, our inflated pride, and our platform of feeling justified. If we want to maintain harmony, there are times we must compromise, or simply open our hearts and arms and say this disagreement is not as important as our relationship. However, there are those moments when the wrong is so grievous that the "sorry" becomes a process. Infidelity, physical abuse, stealing, habitual irresponsibility, and continual neglect or disrespect requires more than the obligatory "I am sorry." Then unswerving actions will be required to elicit trust in the words "I am sorry" and give them authentic meaning once again.

- *Learn to say "I am sorry," and promise to follow up with behavior that demonstrates you mean the words you offer up as an olive branch. I have learned one hard lesson: if there are those in your life who say they are sorry repeatedly, but never follow through, you may have to expect less from them, or consider them toxic to your well-being.*

- *When saying you are sorry, do not qualify it with a "but" or "and" or a "furthermore." Just say you are sorry and be true.*

- *If one "I am sorry" does not start the healing process, write a letter, send a card, or make a personal gift. Sew it, knit it, bake it, and include a note. It can just be a simple message saying you value the other individuals, and miss them, and love them. Acknowledge that you understand how you hurt them by either letting them down or criticizing them or forgetting to show up for a luncheon date—whatever the issue might be. If over time you know that the issue lies with the other person's inability to forgive, forgive yourself and move on.*

For You, I Wish

The Dignity of Jeepers

They call her Jeepers, a name she inherited some sixty years ago. When I entered her room, I was moved by emotion; words could not prepare me for her disturbing condition as she slumped uncomfortably in her chair. Feeling uncomfortable in my own skin, I spoke quietly to her, but her vacant stare offered no response. I traveled far to be in her presence, inspired by her story. It had been many years since the thief we call Alzheimer's crept into her life, robbing her of everything, only leaving the physical to endure endless suffering—leaving no hope, no cure, and devastating those who loved her so dearly. Here she breathed, living in misery, stripped of her dignity, yet no one I had met before her was more deserving of self-respect or the respect of others. She had witnessed the vicious crimes of her disease in her own mother before her. She was aware that a stranger would enter her mind, diminishing her grace before she would vanish altogether into her own silence. She was fully aware of it all, yet she asked her family, for the sake of finding a cure, to tell her story.

Footage of her demise has been witnessed by countless people, awakening the need for change; her selfless courage to make a difference has done just that, made a difference. . . . Her caretakers moved her to the bed and she immediately curled into a fetal position as if desperately trying to return to a place of warmth and safety. I moved to the bed with her and curled at her feet. Over time a peace, a comfort, overtook me. There I read to her, I rubbed her aching body, and sang her a lullaby. In those moments, I fell in love with this great woman, honored by the opportunity to show my gratitude. For you, I wish the dignity of Jeepers.

"Still, there were 'kisses from the angels,'
moments when Mom would look
right in my eyes and squeeze my hand
as if to say, 'I'm here darling.'"

—LEEZA GIBBONS

❊ Reflection ❊

When living in Los Angeles, our children attended a private school in West Hollywood where I met Barbara and Leeza. I had seen Leeza on television many times in the past, and it would be unfair not to admit that I was a little nervous when talking to her. However, when I learned that her mother was not well, I forgot about all those awkward feelings and spoke to her as I would speak to any woman in the face of losing her mother. We talked a lot about the pain I had experienced with the loss of my mom and what it was like for her having her mother so ill.

As with Barbara, I felt our mothers brought us together, and I really wanted to meet Leeza's mom. After I spoke to Leeza about it, I went home and talked it over with my husband. He supported the idea, so within two weeks I flew from Connecticut down to South Carolina, rented a car, and headed to the nursing home to meet Jeepers. I will always remember the special time I spent with her, and I am very thankful for the support from those who encouraged me to take the opportunity. Leeza's mother passed away ten days after my visit. It is only appropriate that Leeza take over from here and write the reflection to this Wish.

Love, Tricia

It was bewildering at its best, and unbearable most of the time. The questions that ran through my thoughts about my mother as she faded, memory by memory, from our grasp, would often take on an echo that made the pain of the ponder even worse.

What is she thinking? Is she in pain? Is she afraid? Did she feel embarrassed, humiliated, angry? Is "she" still in there? When my dad, my siblings, and our children would speak with her, we tried to seem normal and carry on the relationship we had always enjoyed with her. But without her easy laugh and the quick hug, there was no surface for our words to bounce off, and we fell into that stilted, forced "fake" kind of banter that only served to make us feel as embarrassed as we assumed she was.

Still, there were "kisses from the angels," moments when Mom would look right in my eyes and squeeze my hand as if to say, "I'm here, darling." It was after those moments that I would again be haunted by the question, "Is she locked up inside of her tangled brain, still the same strong southern steel magnolia the kids called JG, short for Jean Gibbons?" Mom always wanted to have grand-kids, but never wanted to be called Grandmom or any version of that! Even those who didn't know her well knew that she was once a powerful voice of independence and someone who presented an almost impossible balance between vulnerability and strength. Those were the qualities that prompted her to "show up for her life" in ways that were counter to others of her generation. Those were the qualities that stirred her resolve and prompted her to ask me to tell her story and "make it count."

She was forgetting, but she did not want to be forgotten. I used her inspiration and her spirit to create our nonprofit organization, The Leeza Gibbons Memory Foundation, and our signature pro-gram, Leeza's Place. It's what our family wished we had during our struggle: a supportive place where caregivers can become educated and empowered to navigate through their challenging course.

That was the woman Tricia knew about when she asked if it was okay with me for her to fly to South Carolina and visit with my mom, who now lived every day vacant and silent. To me, it was as if all the things Mom had not found time to think about until now were surrounding her energy field, keeping most people at a distance. But Tricia is not most people. How many of your friends would fly on their own time and their own dime to visit your mother they had never met, much less your mother diminished by dementia? I told Tricia, honestly and from my heart, that I thought it was lovely that she wanted to see Mom. I really did not think she would. There are so many lessons in this one action. My friend Tricia listened to her instinct, she took action, and she let that be enough.

Doing the thing that makes you uncomfortable usually offers the greatest chance at growth. I love Eleanor Roosevelt's advice to do one thing every day that scares you. Did it scare Tricia to take the action to see my mom? She had spoken on the phone with my father and had received his blessing for the visit as well, but I have to believe that when she walked into the Lowman Home, the skilled nursing facility where mom lived, and walked down the hall to my mother's room, she must have felt uncomfortable. Or maybe she did not.

I believe we rarely regret the things we do in life, only those things we fail to do. Tricia wanted to meet my mother while she was alive. She called me from the nursing home to describe the scene, Mom's mood, what she was wearing. I felt comforted by the notion that Mom would sense that love had entered the room. I saw an episode of *Oprah* with a brain surgeon who had a stroke. It was an ironic fate that gave her intimate knowledge during her years of recovery, which changed the way she lived her life and the way she treated her patients. It allowed her the kind of knowing that can only come from experiencing something. The doctor said even though she could not communicate with everyone who gathered around her after the stroke, she knew their intentions and felt their energy. She wrote a book about it and said that we all must be accountable for what we bring to any situation. I knew that Tricia would bring soothing energy of love to Mom. I thought about how many chances I may have had to do that for others in my life and had left it undone, distracted by the feeling of being uncomfortable.

What Tricia did next was really beautiful. It was a bold, physical move that many of you reading this right now may have never done with your own mothers as an adult. She climbed into bed and curled up next to my mother. It was an intimate gesture that demonstrated Tricia's commitment to her own personal growth and to her quest to discover the truth about our capacity for human kindness.

At the Governor and First Lady's conference on women in Long Beach this year, my friend and mentor Maria Shriver spoke of a moment that had scared her. I smiled as I sat in the audience and heard her describe the scene. It was when she got into bed with her mother, Eunice Shriver, and risked the awkwardness, the loss of control, and the fear of intimacy that comes when our mothers are no longer towers of physical and emotional strength. This is the moment when we recognize the wounded little girls inside of us.

I learned a lot from Tricia's act of love. She showed that love is an action. Tricia made it a verb. I also discovered that pushing past the judgments that others place on us, or that we put upon ourselves, creates the perfect condition for growth. Intimate moments shared between people require that both sides are dedicated to allowing the exchange to be perfect, no matter how it unfolds. Life is most profound when we can give up the need to know what happens, the need to have an answer, or even to form the perfect questions.

"Life is most profound when we can
give up the need to know what happens,
the need to have an answer, or even
to form the perfect questions."

"She was forgetting, but she did
not want to be forgotten."

—LEEZA GIBBONS

Words and Actions from Barbara

"If there's anything I can do to help, just let me know." How often have we heard these words uttered in times of pain, loss, or crisis, and similarly, recall how we find ourselves offering this verbal kneejerk reaction to someone's difficult situation? For those of us who would truly like to help heal or support a family member, a colleague, or even an acquaintance, I suggest asking yourself to go beyond merely saying the words, and instead act on them. How wonderful a world it would be if all the lovely intentions were translated into deeds of action and change.

The Dignity of Jeepers is an example of a grand act of love and friendship that was fulfilled.

If you can physically be with others, go be with them. Clearly and directly ask them, "What can I do right now, at this very moment, that would be of the greatest help?" If they have no answers, find your own.

- *Fix something around the house. Even changing a light bulb helps.*

- *Run an errand: make a stop at the cleaners or post office for your friend. Does she have library books or DVDs that need to be returned? Pick up a few extra items for her if you are buying your own groceries.*

- *Help her children with their homework if you can. Make sure they do their chores. Providing a sense of normalcy can be very comforting in difficult times. Find ways to entertain her children; it will brighten her day.*

- *Walk your friend's dog, feed the other pets, or take them to the vet's office.*

- *Help cook dinner, set the table, wash the dishes, or take out the garbage.*

- *When there is a loss of a loved one, family member, or friend, be helpful and caring in any way you can. Offer to accompany your friend to the mortuary, help her with the details of printing a tribute with a photo and poem for the funeral, or the organization of the food for the memorial. The breadth of involvement depends on your relationship, finances, and time. Assess the situation carefully; you will see places you can help. Be proactive but not intrusive. Loving and capable women are appreciated in difficult situations.*

For You, I Wish

Your Eternal Mother

The rhythm of her heart soothed you long before you took your first breath of air. Her arms cradled you, her kisses smothered you. She held your hand, tied your shoes, brushed your hair. When you were scared, she reassured you; when you were sad, she comforted you. She knew you better than you knew yourself. She is your mother. Tonight you are asked to say good-bye to her, a quest too grand to comprehend. We are never ready to say good-bye to our mothers, regardless of age, for we are all the child looking up into her eyes when it is time to depart. She cannot hold you now. She cannot nurture your bleeding heart or wipe the tears from your swollen eyes.

Mother Nature knew we would all have to say good-bye to our mothers one day and that this departure would redefine our being and leave us hollow inside, so she gifted all of her children with maternal love—maternal love to share with one another when a mother must go. Your mother has wrapped her arms around many others in times of grief and heartache; now let them wrap their arms around you. Find your mother's love in all who love you. See her eyes twinkle through a baby's smile, feel her wisdom in a friend's devotion. In a field of daisies, rest your voice and look to the sky; remember the smell of her skin, the softness in her touch. The way her kiss took away the pain of a scraped knee, the way her voice centered your world. As you feel her so close to you, let the rhythm of her heart soothe you once more and you will come to realize that you started off as one and became two. Now you are one again, and this time it is she who lies within you, for she will forever be in your heart.

"Mother Nature knew we would
all have to say good-bye to our mothers
one day . . . so she gifted all of her
children with maternal love . . ."

—Tricia LaVoice

❋ Reflection ❋

I was thinking of this Wish the other night while watching the twenty-two-year-old Canadian ice skater accept her bronze metal only days after the sudden death of her mother. The audience thundered with applause as families across the world tuned in. It was hard to imagine what she could possibly be feeling. Tears streaming down my face, hurting for this young girl, I wondered if there is an age when it becomes easier to lose our mothers. I was thirty-one when my mother died and not even close to being done needing her love and guidance. I thought of all my friends who have lost their mothers, thought about their ages, and wondered if any of them had an easier time with their loss.

Vastly unfair, Leeza in the mid years of her life had to experience the loss of her mother twice. First, when the dreadful disease of Alzheimer's silenced her mother to her own world, and then again, when her body shut down. Barbara is in her mid-fifties; her mother is eighty-four. I think about when Barbara will have to say good-bye to her mother and know it will be just as painful and difficult for her as it was for me.

After my mother died, I do not know if I was even conscious of it, but I managed to seek out maternal figures over the next decade to help fill that vast, dark hole of sadness. I have many friends my age, but over the years I befriended a handful of women, all about ten to twenty years older than myself, and one more maternal than the next. They check in on me when I am not well, follow my children's achievements, and make sure I am being good to Rich. They are kind and gentle women, and the simple words of endearment they use when talking to me—"Honey, Sweetie, Sweetheart"—warm my heart all day long. When you do not have maternal love, you are so appreciative to receive it.

My friend Terese bears a striking resemblance to my mother. I found her soon after my mother died, and then Barbara years later. They stepped into my life with such love and devotion that it prompted me to write a novel, Pieces of My Mother, which sits on my desk. In the book, I question whether my mother had sent these beautiful women to me, knowing how badly I was in need of maternal love. They were there at Grandparents' Day events, birthdays, and holidays *for my children. They make sure I am taking care of myself so that I can take better care of my family. They make me feel like I belong. When a mother is lost, we cannot replace her or stop the pain. However, we can reach inside of ourselves and love one another with the kindness of a maternal heart.*

"As a child my mother always told me, 'I am always with you, right there on your shoulder, and I always will be.' I often find myself in moments of doubt, or concern, whispering to my right shoulder."

—BARBARA LAZAROFF

Words and Actions from Barbara

My mother, Ellie, lost her mom at the age of four, and sadly, does not retain any memory of her except for stories others have related. Yet my mother, who did not have a caring relationship with her stepmother, miraculously revealed a deep reservoir of love and abiding strength while raising my two brothers and me. She demonstrated enormous resiliency, patience, courage, and humor in the most difficult of times; and we always felt safe and cherished at home. She was my greatest cheerleader, always on my team, whether I won or lost. She taught me the importance of always trying my best, never giving up, being a team player when appropriate, and yet gave me the confidence to shine on my own with my best efforts and consistent dedication to a goal. I am blessed to still have her in my life.

Although I cannot completely understand the loss, I try to be very supportive when a friend has to say good-bye to her mother. I cared for my dearest girlfriend in the hospital and at home, and back to the hospital once again before she passed away. The complexity of feelings: tragic, enduring love; denial and disbelief; and finally, acceptance, permeated the room for weeks and weeks. Three generations stood guard. My dying friend protectively watched her identical twin daughters and her mother; her mother watched her extraordinary daughter suffer and ebb away, tenderly trying to shelter her granddaughters. My goddaughters were bereft in the knowledge that their mom was leaving them, yet they held strong for their mother and grandmother. The tribe of friends held vigil; she was never alone. I slept in the hospital room, and then one day at 4:06 P.M. she left us, and we cried and cried and cried, and held each other close. Another mother had left her children far too soon.

Some thoughts on providing solace:

- *Lie on the bed with your friend or sit next to her on the couch and let her weep. Do not try to contain the grief. Listen to her reminisce; hear her pain.*

- *If she needs and wants physical contact, hold her hands and embrace her.*

- *Find a picture of her with her mother and put it in a locket.*

- *Call your friend on the first Mother's Day, her mother's birthday, and the anniversary of her mother's passing.*

- *Mail a weekly greeting card. If you knew her mother well, relate a memory.*

- *Send a box filled with her favorite treat, a fruit arrangement or nuts (something healthy to fortify her), an uplifting DVD to watch, or a CD with calming music. Aromatherapy can be a spirit lifter or relaxer as well, as can essential oils with lovely scents, or a basket with lotions and bath salts.*

- *If you live nearby, go sit together and read to her. Pick an uplifting book, something light, and each night read a few chapters to her.*

- *Wish for her every day. Start your morning by sending her a simple "Wish of the Day." It does not have to be poetic, just thoughtful.*

- *When we lose those we love, we do not want them to be forgotten. When your friend is ready to talk about memories and moments that she shared with her mother, be there for her and reinforce her healing process.*

- *If over time your friend becomes overly reclusive; increasingly less verbal with friends and family; or starts having sleep, eating, or work issues, it might be necessary to suggest a bereavement group or private counseling. Help her follow through by either driving her there, attending with her, or attempting an intervention.*

"A woman is like a tea bag,
you can't tell how strong she is until
you put her in hot water."

—ELEANOR ROOSEVELT, FORMER FIRST LADY

"My mom was my greatest cheerleader,
always on my team whether I won or lost."

—BARBARA LAZAROFF

For You, I Wish

A Bow Goodnight—Tribute to Robert Graham

"Sculpt me a woman," you challenged my boy. I walked today through the winter's trees thinking of you, unsure of how a mother shows her respect to a man who has touched the soul of her child. I walked today through the winter's trees crying about you, not sure how a mother tells her son that his mentor has passed. The trees surrounding me were bare of their leaves, their branches were brittle, and their bark had darkened in the frigid air. Yet, in the winter of my sadness, I see what I could not see before: a bird's nest perched high above the ground, once hidden in foliage, now clear to my eyes, a haven a mother so carefully sculpted to nurture her young. Her nest rests now, its work complete; but the life it held, the life it touched, is off soaring the skies before it, too, will pause and sculpt a haven for its young. . . .

"Sculpt me a woman," you challenged my boy, the man with the hands gifted from heaven who now is soaring the skies. Your work is done, yet you live on in the hands and heart of my child and in the hands and hearts of all you have nurtured and touched.

For you, Robert Graham, I bow and wish you goodnight.

"Her nest rests now, its
work complete, but the life
it held is off soaring the skies."

—Tricia LaVoice

❋ Reflection ❋

I met Robert Graham, the great sculptor, at an art show that Barbara and I attended shortly before my family moved from Los Angeles to Connecticut. I was aware that Robert Graham's work could be found in many prominent places across America, from the Roosevelt Memorial in D.C. to the Olympic Gateways in Los Angeles. However, witnessing his work firsthand was breathtaking.

As we left the show, Barbara introduced me to Robert, and told him I had a son, Jack, who had shown a talent for sculpting. I asked him if he had any advice for me and he replied, "Tell him to give it away."

So we did just that. I spent a fortune at the art store buying clay, and Jack sculpted every chance he had and then gave his creations away as gifts. Two years later, I wrote Robert Graham a letter. I told him I was a mom from Connecticut with a ten-year-old son interested in art. I never mentioned that I had met him earlier or that I was friendly with people in Los Angeles that he might know. I simply asked if I could bring my son by his studio while visiting L.A. His wonderful assistant replied promptly with a good time to stop by the studio.

Weeks later, I sat still while Jack was given a firsthand tour of the studio. As we went to leave, Jack handed Robert a piece of art he had made for him out of clay. Robert held it in his hands, looking down at Jack with so much emotion in his eyes. Then he excused himself for a moment and returned with one of his bronze pieces to give to Jack. This was the beginning of their sweet protégé/mentor relationship, the beginning of their respect for one another as artists.

Over the next two years, Jack flew to Los Angeles a couple of times to attend Robert's art showings and to visit him at his studio. During one of those visits, Jack asked Robert what his favorite animal was so he could sculpt it for him. Without hesitation, Robert replied, "Woman." Jack was challenged, so I came up with an idea and headed to the video store to rent <u>The Addams Family</u> movie starring Angelica Huston, Robert's wife for over fifteen years. Jack carefully sculpted a little Morticia Addams and mailed her off to Robert with a note saying, "Here is your favorite woman."

What touched me the most about Robert Graham's role in Jack's life was how unconditionally he gave to Jack. When we visited the studio, I would sit to the side and listen as Jack asked endless questions and Robert so patiently answered them. He took Jack under his wing, sharing so much of himself but never asking for anything in return. One holiday, Robert made his friends and family art pieces out of clay and sent one to Jack with a note thanking him.

When Robert unexpectedly passed, telling Jack was one of the hardest things I have ever had to do. He was devastated. We decided to take him out of school and fly him to be with Barbara in Los Angeles to attend Robert Graham's memorial so that he could pay his respects to the man, the teacher, the mentor who touched his heart ever so deeply, where he will always remain.

Words and Actions from Barbara

When we respect someone's artistry, intelligence, character, and athletic prowess and they in return allow us to see ourselves through their eyes, filled with confidence in our potential, we are changed forever for the better. The loss of someone who has shaped our life by providing us with inspiration is a tremendous bereavement, particularly for a young person. Usually a loss of this magnitude occurs with someone we have forged a long relationship with over years of shared experiences, such as a parent, an extended family member, or a longtime teacher or friend. The situation with Tricia's son, Jack, and Robert Graham was an unusual one. I had suggested that young Jack meet a professional artist, a genius sculptor such as Robert, because Jack's reason for being was so completely entwined with his clay creations. When Robert passed away, his death was devastating for Jack, who thought he would have many more years of mentoring, and an ongoing friendship with the master.

Tricia was conflicted as to whether to tell Jack right away, and how to relate the sad news. Robert Graham's funeral was refined and would have done justice to a saint. Jack and I attended together; it was proper closure for a man of such talent and vision and an important moment for Jack, his special time to say good-bye. He brought a white dove he had been sculpting to give to Angelica Huston, Robert's widow. Tricia, as a sensitive mother, flew Jack across the country, knowing this was essential for her son.

We also see how sometimes the length of time alone does not reflect the measure of impact someone can have on another's life. It reminds us that every interaction we have with another human being can be very powerful in both a positive or negative way. We must be mindful, especially with children, when we share our time with them. We can all be powerful influences in the life of a child, and we need to be accountable and conscientious with our words and actions.

- *Never underestimate your influence on a child's life; be a mentor.*

- *Indulge the child protégé's passions and interests; if he loves to paint or sculpt, take him to museums, art galleries, and art openings where he can meet artists.*

- *If the child loves music, then escort him or her to a variety of different concerts. If you search, you will find free ones in your community. If you can afford music lessons for the child, encourage their practicing by listening and applauding their progress; (even if initially the listening is difficult on the ears).*

- *If it is in your budget, buy dance lessons for the dancer, writing classes for the budding journalist, or get the child a journal, and encourage writing every day, offering to read the work if the child is comfortable sharing. The internet and library offer many books on creative writing techniques.*

- *Encourage the young scientist by visiting the planetarium, the local aquarium, or seaside; perhaps there is a guest speaker or a lecture of particular interest in your area you can both attend. If the child is fascinated by the ocean and interested in marine biology, going snorkeling is great fun, and scuba diving is a great sport to learn.*

- *Communicate to these children that you are proud of their efforts and believe in their abilities. A good mentor is encouraging and inspiring.*

- *Include them in activities with your family.*

- *Always be open to discussing the loss of a child's mentor, even if it is a painful process for you. If the mentor was your mom or dad, your child's fond memories will help heal you both.*

One of the most gratifying aspects of my life is the relationship I have forged with all my goddaughters. One of them I had met at age five: I helped support her at certain moments through a difficult childhood, and her school years. She honored me by asking if I would be the matron of honor at her wedding. She has now earned her Ph.D., and recently became a mother. Each of my goddaughters has their own distinct personality, intellect, and charm; they have all enriched my life.

This quote resonates with me more deeply,
the longer I am on this earth:

"We make a living by what we get,
we make a life by what we give."

—SIR WINSTON CHURCHILL,
FORMER PRIME MINISTER OF ENGLAND

For You, I Wish

Honor

I sat off to the side waiting while a woman next to me fumbled through her bag. The sounds of a father trying to calm his child competed with the typical hustle and bustle of the airport on a Tuesday afternoon. My eye took notice of three women hurrying from window to window, anxiously awaiting the arrival of an aircraft. Obviously sisters, they giggled and pointed as the welcoming signs they made pressed against the window. Repeatedly, they asked one another, "Do you see her, do you see her?" Their excitement was endearing. I wondered curiously, was it a fourth sister they awaited? Their mother? But it became apparent that one of the women had more at stake than the other two. She bit her nails, wrapped her arms around her stomach, and paced at a feverish rate. Was it her daughter, maybe returning from college, maybe on the eve of her wedding?

As their plane arrived, I noticed I was not the only one in the waiting area giving them an audience; many of us watched with anticipation. One by one, men and women, boys and girls, deplaned. Finally, a flight attendant reached the area and assured them, "She is on her way." The mother's expression mystified me, tears swelling in her eyes as she cupped her face with her shaking hands, but then it became clear. Her daughter appeared. She was beautiful, a girl in her late teens, maybe early twenties, with long strawberry blonde hair and a face covered in freckles—her uniform, shades of green and brown that are worn only by the U.S. military. She dropped her gear as she reached out and buried her face in the chest of her mother. The waiting area burst into applause. The older gentlemen went first, but immediately, one by one, the waiting room stood. Tears flowed down many faces as this brave young soldier desperately tried to stay strong.

Someone yelled, "It's okay, soldiers cry too!" and her body shook with emotion. A feeling of oneness, of unity, swept through the room as we all paid tribute to the example of courage and sacrifice before us. The applause held steady as the mother and daughter released their embrace, but what happened next I will remember for the rest of my life. The young woman who risked her life for us and whose mind now holds unfathomable memories, walked straight through the crowd. She never once stopped and asked anything of me or anyone else; she asked for nothing in return.

I wish for you, the depth of this soldier's, and all those in service, honor.

"I was envious of her passion for
a cause—a love of her country, that
she would risk injury, even her life,
to be a soldier."

—Tricia LaVoice

❋ Reflection ❋

No matter how many times I read this Wish, tears come to my eyes when thinking about that day. I imagine not a moment goes by when a mother is not thinking about her child who is in the service. I think about how many times a day, or even a week, I stop and think about our young soldiers, the sacrifice they are making for my country, my family, and my children; and I certainly know it is not nearly enough. Rarely do I think about the sacrifice their mothers and fathers are making, but this day shed light into the personal lives of military family life.

What this brave soldier taught me as she walked by us, her head held high, her eyes wet with tears, was the meaning of honor. I, for one, have never held such honor in my heart. In an odd way, I was almost envious of her passion for a cause, a love of her country—that she would risk injury, even her life, to be a soldier. And more beautiful than her willingness to fight for her cause was her willingness to do so without asking for anything in return from those of us she is defending. Yes, the government pays them for their service, but no one risks their lives, leaves their families, and lives in stressful conditions just for a paycheck. Honor, not money, gives them the strength to see it through another night.

It was wonderful to feel the vibration of applause run through the airport for this soldier, to watch the entire sitting area became one in emotion as we witnessed the raw display of love shared between this mother and daughter as they held on to one another in pure relief and gratitude. But the sacrifice is not just hers; her mother held on to her, letting out sounds of joy that you knew came from the depth of her soul. To both the soldier and her mother, to all of our soldiers and all of their families, I would like to say thank you!

"These men and women
courageously defend our freedom.
They are all someone's beloved child; they
leave their families to protect ours.
Honor them, thank them,
remember them, always."

—Barbara Lazaroff

Words and Actions from Barbara

Families with loved ones in the military experience stressful separation, fears, and moments of loneliness. Upon their return, many members of the armed forces experience a difficult reentry into society. Some are physically or emotionally disabled, and their lives are greatly altered. Some individuals can be rehabilitated, and others who have admirably served our country find that their marriages dissolve and there are no work opportunities.

We should honor our military personnel abroad and at home and remember that their service safeguards our freedom. There are countless ways we can show our respect and gratitude to members of the armed forces—not only by supporting them, but by supporting their families as well.

- *When you see a serviceman or woman out in public, bring your hand to your heart and look him or her in the eye as you nod your head; if you are not this demonstrative, simply smile.*

- *If it is obvious that he or she is with family, say thank you to all of them if the situation permits. This may feel awkward, but remember, a serviceman or woman risks his or her life for your life. Their family makes many sacrifices for your family's safety. However, be respectful of boundaries; if the moment appears intensely personal, be respectful and do not interfere.*

- *If you are in a line at the store, at the bank, or at the movies and see a member of the military, ask him or her to please go first, express your feelings, and tell them it would be your honor.*

- *Make cookies; drawings; or write letters with your kids, the neighborhood children, or a local school, and bring them to a VA nursing home. You can also send these items abroad to our troops.*

- *You can support a particular veteran, or share your time and resources with a few, by purchasing or loaning books, music CDs, or writing letters; delivering home-cooked meals every week or once a month. Get a group of friends together, create a "Support a Veteran" club, and rotate visiting days, talents, and resources. By asking your friends to join you in this gesture of concern and appreciation for our vets, you can rally the spirit of the entire community. Bring together people who can teach the veterans new skills and stimulating hobbies: photography, painting, computer programming, creative writing, music—maybe a guitar teacher can attend. For fun, try darts, Scrabble, or Monopoly. Perhaps there is a person in your group who can play the violin or piano, sing, or is genuinely funny. You need to know if the vets are welcoming of your involvement in their lives—some may be too private, or need or desire solitude.*

- *Invite a serviceman or woman's family over for a barbecue or dinner, or a weekend of relaxation. If you have a pool or garden, swim or plant flowers—these are nurturing activities. Ask them to make themselves at home and read or just look at the sky and trees. You can watch a movie together, or if you have a table, play ping-pong, chess, checkers, or cards. Entertain their children with creative projects at home; or take them to a zoo, park, or the planetarium.*

- *If the dad is in the service and currently out on active duty, perhaps your son, husband, or brother can play ball with their son. If the mother is in military service and absent, the children may need some maternal love and support; take the girl for a manicure or hairstyling. Perhaps the boy needs a haircut, a cool T-shirt, or just a friendly, fun trip to an ice cream parlor to sit, talk, and relax.*

- *Ask the parent who is at home what support their child might need at school; offer your time or skills for an event or project that requires an additional adult.*

- *If you are a business owner, advertise for veterans, and hire qualified applicants. Vets are great employees. They are respectful, organized, skilled, and disciplined.*

- *Just listening to the spouse, the children, or the parents of a serviceman or woman can be very comforting for the family.*

- *For further insights, visit internet sites such as **military .com** for additional ideas on how you can offer your support.*

"How important it is for us to recognize and celebrate our heroes and she-roes!"

—MAYA ANGELOU, POET AND AUTHOR

Wishes
to Share

(We've repeated three of the wishes here
for you to cut out and share with others.)

For You, I Wish

My Love and Gratitude

Life holds precious gifts for us, unfolding them as we call on them. All are treasures, yet there is one immeasurable in value to the heart. This gift is living within the essence of all women, regardless of age, or whether they have given birth or not: the gift to nurture, to value, to bestow maternal love. I ask, but what is a mother? She is the one who lifts you when your heart is aching, the one who finds you when you have lost "you," the one who stands silent so you can sing. She cares for you in illness, celebrates you in triumph, and encourages you in hardship.

You are my friend; when I am down, you lift me up; when I am lost, you find me, and when I achieve, you celebrate me. I wish for you my love and gratitude.

For You, I Wish

Your Eternal Mother

The rhythm of her heart soothed you long before you took your first breath of air. Her arms cradled you, her kisses smothered you. She held your hand, tied your shoes, brushed your hair. When you were scared, she reassured you; when you were sad, she comforted you. She knew you better than you knew yourself. She is your mother. Tonight you are asked to say good-bye to her, a quest too grand to comprehend. We are never ready to say good-bye to our mothers, regardless of age, for we are all the child looking up into her eyes when it is time to depart. She cannot hold you now. She cannot nurture your bleeding heart or wipe the tears from your swollen eyes.

Mother Nature knew we would all have to say good-bye to our mothers one day and that this departure would redefine our being and leave us hollow inside, so she gifted all of her children with maternal love—maternal love to share with one another when a mother must go. Your mother has wrapped her arms around many others in times of grief and heartache; now let them wrap their arms around you. Find your mother's love in all who love you. See her eyes twinkle through a baby's smile, feel her wisdom in a friend's devotion. In a field of daisies, rest your voice and look to the sky; remember the smell of her skin, the softness in her touch. The way her kiss took away the pain of a scraped knee, the way her voice centered your world. As you feel her so close to you, let the rhythm of her heart soothe you once more and you will come to realize that you started off as one and became two. Now you are one again, and this time it is she who lies within you, for she will forever be in your heart.

For You, I Wish

A River's Love

All the river knows is to journey home, letting nothing stand in her way. In times of drought, she flows with calmness, low to the ground, not rousing the earth. In times of surge, she roars, rapidly racing her course. Place an obstacle in her way and she will overcome it with her determination and spirit squeezing under, over, and around the largest of boulders, the smallest of debris. All she knows is to journey home.

All I know is to love you, letting nothing stand in my way. In times of struggle, I will remain gentle, providing you with clarity. In times of conflict, I will move swiftly, softening your ache. If you detach from me, I will tenderly wait. If you place an obstacle in my way, I will trounce it; and if you find resentment and fury with me, I will humble myself. All the river knows is to journey home, as all I know is to love you. For you, I wish a river's love.

ACKNOWLEDGMENTS

I have been blessed to have had two of the most incredible, loving parents, Bill and Pat Lanahan, to guide me and love me. Although our time together was far too short, they remain alive in my heart. I am deeply grateful to them now and forever; I am a better wife, mother, and friend because of their tender wisdom and guidance.

My intention when writing the first Wish was to return the love and support to my dear friend Barbara Lazaroff that she had offered me. I never expected a Wish to be read by anyone else. How the Wishes have grown is just another example of how Barbara's love reaches so many. I thank her from the bottom of my heart for that love.

I would like to thank beautiful Leeza Gibbons, who would not stop believing in me until I believed in myself as well. Her love, wisdom, and guidance has taught me so much over the years. In addition, thanks to the wonderful BobbyX and everyone over at *Hollywood Confidential.*

Deep love and appreciation goes to all my wonderful friends whose love and support has held me through the hard times and lifted me in the good times—those wiser in years, and the younger, powerful generation from Yardley to Marin, Manhattan to Los Angeles, to Avon.

This book would never have come to fruition without the encouragement and support from a few special friends: Bill, Dan, Pam, Dorothy, Sondra, Arthur, Leigh Ann, Terese, Sheila, Becky, Julie, Lynn, and my steadfast Martha.

Furthermore, to my wonderful family and in-laws including the most amazing mother herself, sister Elizabeth. My love and respect for her is boundless.

And then there are my remarkable children: Olivia, Billy, Jack, and Bobby, whose love sustains me. My sun rises and sets in their smiles. And finally, to the love of my life who experiences the best and worst of me—my loving husband Rich. As the saying goes, "Behind every successful woman is herself," but I could not have done any of this without him at my side. Rich, thank you for sharing your life with me.

— Love, Tricia

I have so many warm, wise, courageous, patient, supportive, and witty women in my sisterhood who have guided me over the years on the ever-unpredictable pathways and passages of life. I have gleaned so much deep knowledge and acceptance from remarkable women of all ages who have enlightened me, uplifted me in my most painful days, and danced with me in times of triumph. The laughter and memories we share illuminate my days. There are many brilliant, warm, and philanthropic ladies I have encountered in my thirty years of business and charity work. Their lessons of life are now mine as well. I admire them.

I thank my entire family, but above all I give profound thanks to my role model and very best friend—my mother, Ellie, who shared my joyful moments of accomplishment, but supported me as steadfastly in my times of uncertainty.

Thanks, Dad and Mom, for giving me life and being such loving grandparents.

Big love to my perfect "in their own unique ways" sons, Cameron and Byron. You are both the light and loves of my life. Now and always. I am proud to be the mother of such fine young men.

Deepest adoration and respect for my longtime beau John Hanwell for always infusing laughter into our lives and for having "arms around me" during all the peaks and valleys. You are a man of integrity. Sharing your wonderful mom and family with me has been a precious gift.

I extend thanks to friends Kay Collins and Muna Deriane in my office who read, reread, and reread yet again.

For my dear spirit sister Sondra Scerca, much gratitude for your sweetly offered suggestions and gentle words. You are with me no matter where you are.

Constant love and loyalty to my darling longtime friends Rosalind Millstone, Lisette Ackerberg, and Eleanor Hedge, all women of a certain age who were always wiser than their many years of experience. They inspire me daily with their strength, courage, and desire to live well and fully every day, even through your most challenging of times.

Gratitude and abiding love to my goddaughters of all ages, who have kept my mind and heart flexible, reminding us every day of life's glorious possibilities.

My love and loyalty, now and always, to my co-author and wonderful friend Tricia LaVoice, who was generous and tenacious in desiring to share this project with me. We venture out now to add a touch of inspiration and support to our sisters—the women who nurture this planet.

— Strength, love, and inspiration, Barbara

Together, we would like to extend a special thank-you to the fabulous CEO of Dupree/Miller & Associates, Jan Miller, for her vision; the wildly intelligent Shannon Marven for her editorial insight; and a bundle of love and admiration to our sweet talented agent Lacy Lynch for her commitment and endless encouragement.

Having the opportunity to work with such an amazing publishing company whose enthusiastic commitment to inspirational books makes a difference in the world has been an honor. In gratitude we thank Reid Tracy, Gail Gonzales, Stacey Smith, Jill Kramer, Christy Salinas, and the rest of the Hay House team.

Extending well-earned appreciation to grammar gurus, ever good-spirited Don LaVoice and eloquent Lea Purwin D'Agostino, who both agree that proper grammar is an art form.

Our thanks go out to Fabio at Doghaus Designs for his creative energy and willingness to work as long as it takes; and to Eric Musser for his marketing skills and vision. Also, thanks to Susan Merlo of Next Level iMedia Marketing for her insight and determination.

~ *Tricia and Barbara*

ABOUT THE AUTHORS

Tricia LaVoice earned a bachelor of science degree in Applied Psychology from California State University, Long Beach, and a master's degree in Educational Psychology from Fordham University.

In her earlier years, she dedicated a substantial amount of time to women's crisis hotlines and is currently engaged in the area of bereavement issues.

Tricia greatly enjoys writing for children and adults. Her first book, *Helmets and Hoses, Toes and Noses,* was released by Orchard Academy Press in July of 2008. Her second book, *Pieces of My Mother,* is currently being reviewed for publication.

Leeza Gibbons has read many of Tricia's Wishes on her nationally syndicated radio program, *Hollywood Confidential.* Tricia's writings can also be found on Leeza's website at **www.Leeza Gibbons.com.**

Tricia lives in the countryside in Avon, Connecticut, with her husband, daughter, and three sons. She is a yoga enthusiast and finds inspiration for her Wishes on many of her long daily walks in nature.

www.tricialavoice.com
www.stfranciscare.org

Restaurateur, philanthropist, and interior designer **Barbara Lazaroff, A.S.I.D.,** is renowned for her innovative restaurant concepts. As president of Imaginings Interior Designs, Inc., Barbara has designed such popular restaurants as the original Spago Hollywood; Spago Beverly Hills; Chinois in Santa Monica and Las Vegas; Eureka, Granita, and other noted dining establishments. She continues her work in the restaurant industry as a co-brander and partner in a multitude of "Wolfgang Puck" business entities and is a member of the Board of Directors of Wolfgang Puck Worldwide.

Barbara's unique concepts and designs have received critical acclaim and numerous awards. Her work has been featured in *Designer's West, Restaurant Hospitality, Elle Décor, Fortune, Interiors, Restaurant/Hotel Design International, Luxe,* and *Vogue.* She has been profiled on CNN, *Women on Top* (a Canadian show about female entrepreneurs), *Good Morning America, Home Show, Public Eye, Interior Motives,* and *West 57th,* among others. In 1991, Barbara was inducted into the prestigious Platinum Circle of design professionals by *Restaurant/Hotel Design International.* She received an honorary degree of Doctor of Business Administration in Hospitality Management from Johnson and Wales University in 1998. In 2000, Barbara was inducted into the National Association of Women Business Owners Millennium Hall of Fame, which noted her leadership and business acumen.

In 1982, Barbara co-founded the annual American Wine and Food Festival, which funds the Puck-Lazaroff Charitable Foundation, whose sole mission is providing key support for the Meals on Wheels Program in L.A. In 1984, she co-founded the annual California Spirit event, which supports the American Cancer Society. Barbara has hosted an annual Spago Passover Seder since 1984, providing hunger relief in the community. Most notable among her many charitable honors are the James Beard Humanitarian Award, the KindredSpirits Humanitarian Award, and the Aviva Family and Children's Services' Spirit of Compassion Award—an organization close to her heart. Barbara recently completed a four-year remodel of one of the Aviva residences. Barbara serves on the Board of Directors of The Friends of Sheba Medical Center, located in Israel.

In addition, Barbara is engaged in a number of organizations that promote women in the hospitality industry, and the political and design arenas. She is one of the founding members of Women Chefs and Restaurateurs. Barbara is on the Board of Governors of Jewish Life Television and a frequent on-air guest, and has recently signed with Fremantle Media for an original TV series. She is also a passionate collector and patron of the arts. Barbara resides in Beverly Hills with her two sons Cameron and Byron, her longtime beau, and a menagerie of pets.

www.barbaralazaroff.com
www.awff.org (American Wine and Food Festival
for Meals on Wheels)
www.calspirit.org (California Spirit Event for the
American Cancer Society)
www.icrfla.org (for Cancer Research and the Rachel Society)
www.avivacenter.org (Aviva Family and Children's Services)
www.zimmermuseum.org (The Zimmer Children's Museum)
www.nawbo.org (National Association of Women Business Owners)
www.womenchefs.org (for women in hospitality)
www.fulfillment.org (Fulfillment Fund for
childhood education programs)
www.shebamed.org (Friends of Sheba Medical Center)
www.bbbs.org (Big Brothers/Big Sisters)

A special thank-you to Jan Miller, Shannon Marven, sweet Lacy Lynch, and the team of Dupree/Miller and Associates for their continual support and tireless efforts.

Hay House Titles of Related Interest

YOU CAN HEAL YOUR LIFE, the movie, starring Louise L. Hay &
Friends (available as a 1-DVD program and an expanded 2-DVD set)
Watch the trailer at: **www.LouiseHayMovie.com**

THE SHIFT, the movie,
starring Dr. Wayne W. Dyer (available as a 1-DVD
program and an expanded 2-DVD set)
Watch the trailer at: **www.DyerMovie.com**

*DR. CHRISTIANE NORTHRUP'S MOTHER-DAUGHTER
WISDOM* **DVD,** by Christiane Northrup, M.D.

*EMPOWERING WOMEN: Every Woman's Guide
to Successful Living,* by Louise L. Hay

*THE LIVES OUR MOTHERS LEAVE US: Prominent Women
Discuss the Complex, Humorous, and Ultimately Loving
Relationships They Have with Their Mothers,* by Patti Davis

*WHAT THEY KNOW ABOUT PARENTING:
Celebrity Moms and Dads Give Us Their Take on Having Kids.*
Interviews by Cindy Pearlman; edited by Jill Kramer

All of the above are available at your local bookstore, or
may be ordered by contacting Hay House (see next page).

We hope you enjoyed this Hay House book. If you'd
like to receive our online catalog featuring additional
information on Hay House books and products, or if you'd
like to find out more about the Hay Foundation, please contact:

Hay House, Inc., P.O. Box 5100, Carlsbad, CA 92018-5100
(760) 431-7695 or (800) 654-5126
(760) 431-6948 (fax) or (800) 650-5115 (fax)
www.hayhouse.com® • www.hayfoundation.org

Published and distributed in Australia by: Hay House
Australia Pty. Ltd., 18/36 Ralph St., Alexandria NSW 2015
Phone: 612-9669-4299 • *Fax:* 612-9669-4144 • www.hayhouse.com.au

Published and distributed in the United Kingdom by:
Hay House UK, Ltd., 292B Kensal Rd., London W10 5BE • *Phone:* 44-20-8962-
1230 • *Fax:* 44-20-8962-1239 • www.hayhouse.co.uk

Published and distributed in the Republic of South Africa by:
Hay House SA (Pty), Ltd., P.O. Box 990, Witkoppen 2068
Phone/Fax: 27-11-467-8904 • www.hayhouse.co.za

Published in India by: Hay House Publishers India,
Muskaan Complex, Plot No. 3, B-2, Vasant Kunj, New Delhi 110 070
Phone: 91-11-4176-1620 • *Fax:* 91-11-4176-1630 • www.hayhouse.co.in

Distributed in Canada by: Raincoast,
9050 Shaughnessy St., Vancouver, B.C. V6P 6E5
Phone: (604) 323-7100 • *Fax:* (604) 323-2600 • www.raincoast.com

Take Your Soul on a Vacation

Visit **www.HealYourLife.com**® to regroup,
recharge, and reconnect with your own magnificence.
Featuring blogs, mind-body-spirit news, and
life-changing wisdom from Louise Hay and friends.

Visit **www.HealYourLife.com** today!